Guide to a
Well-Behaved
Parrot

Third Edition

Mattie Sue Athan

With Full-Color Photographs
Illustrations by Michele Earle-Bridges

BARRON'S

Dedication

To my family.

About the Author

Mattie Sue Athan is one of the most experienced parrot behavior consultants in the world. Since the mid 1970s, she has studied the development and modification of behavior in parrots living as companions with humans. She has won *Amazon.com's* Best Selling Bird Care Book Award, as well as the Oklahoma Writer's Federation, Inc.'s Non-Fiction Best Book award.

Photo Credits

Mattie Sue Athan: pages viii, 6 (top), 42, 51, 73, 88, 94, and 120; Joan Balzarini: pages 10 (top and bottom), 14, 21, and 29; Norvia Behling: pages 9, 22, 24, 53, 65, 95, 99, and 119; Gerry Bucsis and Barbara Somerville: pages 8 (bottom), 30, 63, 122, 123, 127, and 130; Susan Green: pages x, 3, 5, 6 (bottom), 8 (top), 12, 15, 17, 19, 25, 28, 35, 40, 43, 45, 46, 49, 59, 61, 62, 69, 76, 78, 80, 81, 82, 84, 85, 90, 103, and 116; Margaret Salvidar: page 4 (top and bottom); Lynne Vincent: pages ix and 27; and B. Everett Webb: pages 34, 66, 87, and 91.

Cover Photos

Front cover: Getty Images; back cover: Susan Green; inside front cover: Susan Green; inside back cover: Norvia Behling.

All inquiries should be addressed to:
Barron's Educational Series, Inc.
250 Wireless Boulevard
Hauppauge, New York 11788
www.barronseduc.com

Library of Congress Catalog Card No. 2007021623

ISBN-13: 978-0-7641-3667-2
ISBN-10: 0-7641-3667-4

Library of Congress Cataloging-in-Publication Data
Athan, Mattie Sue.
  Guide to a well-behaved parrot / [Mattie Sue Athan] ;
  illustrations by Michele Earle-Bridges. — 3rd ed.
      p. cm.
  Includes bibliographical references and index.
  ISBN-13: 978-0-7641-3667-2 (alk. paper)
  ISBN-10: 0-7641-3667-4 (alk. paper)
  1. Parrots—Behavior. 2. Parrots—Training. I. Title.

SF473.P3A84   2007
636.6´865—dc22   2007021623

Printed in China

9 8 7 6 5 4 3 2 1

Important Note
While every effort has been made to ensure that all information in this text is accurate, up-to-date, and easily understandable, we cannot be responsible for unforeseen consequences of the use or misuse of this information. Poorly socialized or unhealthy parrots may be a danger to humans in the household. Escaped non-native species represent an environmental threat in some places. Outdoor release or unrestricted outdoor flight is absolutely condemned by the ethical parrot keeper. This book recommends that a parrot's wing feathers be carefully trimmed at least three times each year.

Contents

Foreword

Mattie Sue Athan and I started working with parrots about the same time. This was back in the "dark ages" when parrots were just starting to gain popularity as pets in this country. People tried to rely on their intuition to figure out why their pets acted the way they did. Unfortunately, this is often still true. Many owners, who have great expectations of a wonderful relationship with their pet parrot, become completely frustrated as their birds begin to have serious behavioral problems. It seems that no matter what the people try, their parrots still bite, scream, pluck their feathers, hate the owner's spouse, reject any foods but seed, become phobic, refuse to come out of the cage, or won't be tamed. Some owners listen to everyone and try everything. They try to resolve their parrot's behavioral problems with advice intended for breeding birds, dogs, cats, or human children. Their lack of understanding about "parrot psychology" often makes the problems worse.

Fortunately, need usually creates a response. A few people throughout the country who have a great love and special understanding about pet parrots started working to help the frustrated bird owner with their problems. Although Mattie Sue and I started with the same dedication in the mid 1970s, we have just recently become acquainted. Although we often tell different stories and use different words to describe our ideas and techniques, we definitely have the same philosophies. We both feel that taming is based on patiently winning a parrot's trust. We both respect the intelligence of parrots and feel that they need guidance and rules to be good pets. We both believe that parrots are highly reactive to their owner's behavior and that a parrot can't change unless the owner changes. We both share an intense love for the curious comical nature of parrots.

As the editor of the *Pet Bird Report*, a publication featuring behavioral information, I am often asked by parrot owners if there is a good book that deals with pet parrot behavior. So much of the information available is either outdated or deals with parrots as breeders rather than human companions. I am delighted that I can now answer, "Yes, there is a good book that deals with parrot behavior!" and refer them to Mattie Sue Athan's *Guide to a Well-Behaved Parrot.*

Sally Blanchard

Foreword to the Third Edition

A book captures a piece of time. Fact or fiction, the information and style reflect the moment in which the words went onto the paper. For a story or historical account, this is a benefit of written words, allowing us to revisit that day. For instruction or informational volumes, the process doesn't serve "ever" increasing understanding of the subject being studied. A book is written for the audience of the moment with the knowledge available at that moment. As the needs of the audience change with time, a textbook can become outdated, useless.

Unless the book is changed.

When *Guide to a Well-Behaved Parrot* was first published in 1993, the landscape of parrot keeping was completely different from today. We were still seeing many parrots caught wild, which came with quite a different set of problems than those we see today.

Not only were customs and needs different, the way words were used was different. Mattie Sue combined research and personal experience to construct a book that helped a great many parrots and their people.

Then times changed. By the mid 1990's, the U.S. marketplace was forced to become exclusively dependent on aviculture for parrots. It seemed to be fashionable to get a baby bird while it was still handfeeding and raise it yourself. Presumably, the bird would bond with its owner as a "mate," and everyone would be "happy." That line of faulty reasoning spawned a variety of unintended consequences. *Guide to a Well-Behaved Parrot* was updated so that it would address new issues of concern in 1998.

Now it's happening again. Times are changing. Parrot owners are increasingly aware that their birds need to be parrots and not "feathered kids." We are learning that the most well-adjusted parrot is one that uses its "parrotness" successfully in the human environment. So, *Guide to a Well-Behaved Parrot* has been rewritten for the benefit of today's parrot owners, instead of recording how parrots were kept in the past.

Thanks, Mattie Sue, for caring enough about the birds and the people who serve them to invest the huge amount of focus, time, and energy needed to write the same book three times!

Dianalee Deter

Preface

World-wide changes, along with related law and science during the last three decades, have transformed aviculture in the United States. Improved diets, cages, and accessories have enriched one pet parrot's life at a time. However, the most astounding transformation to parrot fancy during this era has been the birds themselves. Instead of autonomous wild-caught parrots, hand-fed domestic-raised chicks now enter their first homes with astounding skills and a few surprising vulnerabilities. Along with lifestyle changes came an education revolution in humans—and with it, companion parrot behavior counseling.

During the time of wild-caught parrots, birds could be found on open perches or in accessible cages in retail settings so that they could interact with potential new families. For better or worse, birds formed responses based on their experiences with strangers—some adept and kind, some not. Eventually, a few more successful, forward-thinking merchants observed that "friendlier" birds were easier to sell, so they found "tamers" to socialize parrots in the store and help clients in their homes. This market-based mandate launched a field of consumer service and scientific research in its support. By the late 1970's Chris Davis, Sally Blanchard, and I had each been drafted in our own special way to serve as behavioral and husbandry consultants for parrots and their people.

The Duke of Bedford's book, *Parrots and Parrot-Like Birds*, written half a century earlier, was then still in print and available for purchase. In 1980, most consumer books addressed species identification or aviculture. Very little information about accommodating pet parrots or managing their behavior was available until 1993, when *Guide to a Well-Behaved Parrot* readied the shelves for a tsunami of similar books to follow. By the end of the twentieth century, most parrot books addressed care, health, or behavioral management of pet birds rather than breeding issues.

During the importation process in the past, parrots had to remain in groups for a 45-day quarantine. They could learn successful adaptive behavior from each other. This period also enabled previously wild animals to observe and acclimate to humans at close range. While some birds didn't survive or remained cautious or even fearful, a surprising number grew hearty and prospered. Many

A wild parrot knows exactly what to do with its beak. (umbrella cockatoo)

down from swinging wire doors. Many lucky parrots found opportunities to eat, drink, make decisions, improvise, reproduce, and, for the most part, run their own darn good, longer-than-wild lives in their new, human-maintained spaces.

Handfed domestic parrots have different life experiences. They probably move to the first new home younger than those wild-caught birds did. A modern parrot might have been purchased even before it hatched or as a naked nestling and visited by new owners during the handfeeding and weaning processes. Once the bird learned to fly and eat independently, it may have gone directly to its new home. So now, if the newly-weaned baby parrot spends all its time with people, how will it learn parrot-like ways?

It's easy for anyone experienced in nurturing puppies and kittens to wind up trying to raise this little feathered "dragon" like a puppy or kitten. Even if the aviculturalist has taken great care to establish exploration and independence during handfeeding and weaning, if a juvenile parrot is over-nurtured, over-supervised, over-ruled, or over-petted in a new home, it can quickly learn to expect—even demand—human touch, human interaction, human participation in all activities, usually by screaming. If once-friendly people withdraw, a lonely, noisy bird can emotionally and behaviorally self-destruct.

Modern parrot behavior counselors support the development of independence in companion parrots, but we

parrots adapted to significant environmental change as though they were born for it. Let's face it: companion parrot life is easy compared to competing in daily life-and-death struggles outdoors. If these birds could survive in sparse, shrinking, challenging wild habitats, they certainly could figure out how to enjoy life in cages where humans were using science to study how to make them happy.

Back during the days of importation into the United States, a parrot-taught parrot knew what to do with wood. Even if there was little or no wood in the cage—perhaps simply a perch—it was chewed. If an exploratory, enterprising bird had toys, it figured out how to play with them. Some pairs took to "singing and climbing walks" in mirror image postures inside their cages or bouncing suspended upside

Living with parrots means expecting the unexpected. (blue and gold macaw)

must also continue our work with cooperation and interaction. And, because we are usually teaching people, not parrots, we have had to acquire increasingly more sophisticated communication skills. No matter where a behavior consultant started in terms of vernacular, those of us who've kept with it have learned to use words with gentler implications. I believe my good fortune—my success as a parrot behavior counselor—has been largely due to the learned use of non-violent, non-judgmental language. Words used today during the process of parrot behavior modification focus increasingly on positive reinforcement—not only toward the birds, but also for their owners, dealers, veterinarians, and other service providers. Rewards for repeating wanted behaviors (patterning successful interactions) remain an industry standard, but I believe efforts to facilitate choice and independence—for all concerned—promise an easier future for indoor parrots and their companions.

A parrot is a bird with a notched upper mandible (beak); a mallet-shaped tongue; and four zygodactyl toes (two opposing two) on each foot. (hyacinth macaw)

Chapter One
Why a Parrot?

Ask a hundred people about life with a parrot and you can expect a hundred different responses. One might say it's as "easy" as stepping over a pile of clothes in the laundry room or another might say it's as easy as coaxing a popcorn hull out of your gums. One might say it's like having a friend for life, while still another might compare it to an extra ex-wife in line for the bathroom.

Some parrots are easier to live with than others, and species is not the primary predictor of successful human/avian relationships. Whether cockatoo or conure, Amazon or Senegal, a particular bird's ability to enjoy behavioral independence seems to be the most crucial element necessary to ensure successful adjustment into human families. This statement is a matter of my opinion, of course. The information in this book comes from almost 30 years of hands-on experience, and that is opinion shaping of the type that can change with time, circumstance, information from new resources, and, of course, more experience.

Living with a parrot is as "easy" as maintaining any other relationship.

Some people stumble into success as a matter of apparent luck, while others struggle with social or interactive skills in efforts to improve their experience. Mostly, enjoying life with a parrot involves tolerance and human willingness to accept and enjoy an exuberant, determined individual with feathers, wings, and a beak.

The Source

Although birds are tidy about their own bodies—regularly bathing, cleaning, and grooming each and every feather—their environments are famously messy. But that's little excuse for a dirty aviary. While even the most meticulous cleaner might occasionally have an off day, the store or breeding facility should be reasonably clean. Bowls should be as close to pristine as possible with clear, fresh-smelling water and little or no debris (some birds like to bathe frequently or dunk food, so their water must be changed often.)

When inquiring about a parrot breeder or dealer's practices and

Warranty and Veterinary Care

A mainstream, Main Street premium companion parrot in the United States comes with a written health guarantee, sometimes as short as three days or as long as a year. This warranty might include a free or pre-paid examination by an avian veterinarian and could provide for treatment or replacement if an illness, injury, or congenital defect was present at the time the bird moved to the new home. Any early veterinary care should be revealed in a medical history provided to the veterinarian of your choice. Although the costs of tests are not usually included in most pre-paid exams, diagnostics can be well worth the investment if a bird proves less hearty than it appeared. Even for a bird in perfect condition, bloodwork or other tests done at this time establish a baseline record for medical evaluation in the future.

Get to know your veterinarian. Look for an experienced, board certified Avian Veterinarian or a member of the Association of Avian Veterinarians. Expect a modern avian practitioner to use diagnostic testing as an integral part of any treatment program. Some very experienced veterinarians may rely on their own practiced ability to evaluate common health issues with physical examination of the bird, its droppings, diet, and other husbandry factors. Especially if your veterinarian diagnoses from physical evaluation, take the bird to the examination room in its cage or, if necessary, take the bird in a carrier and bring used bowls and papers from the cage so that diet, drinking habits, and droppings can be evaluated. In this way, new bird owners are introduced to the very specialized veterinary care necessary for their bouncing bundle of feathers and fits that usually weighs less than a pound. This simple exercise in forethought can save the bird's life in the event of accident or illness down the road.

expertise, expect to be questioned about your own. A handfed baby parrot represents days, weeks, years of feeding, cleaning, and care cycles. A thoughtful breeder has usually invested a big chunk of his or her life in this little bundle of feathers and will want to know your plans, motivations, and intentions toward the bird. Many meticuluous aviculturists maintain a waiting list in order to supply exact numbers of birds needed for a particular season. Many breeders, dealers, stores, and adoption organizations will expect you to have read this book or others, perhaps even requiring multiple visits, volunteerism, and classroom training before being allowed to take one of their birds home.

When seeking a parrot—especially a very young one—you should bathe and change your clothes and shoes before visiting each facility. Be sure to ask permission and expect to handle birds only with supervision. Expect to wash your hands before touching anything. Handle each bird kindly and thoughtfully. This protects the bird (and the interests of their future families) from unexpected mishaps.

Don't tease or allow others to harass the birds. Sudden, unnecessary movements, such as waving hands or arms, can frighten or provoke a reactive parrot. With the occasional exception of goofy large macaws, don't let anybody touch a bird's tail, as even the gentlest tug can terrify some parrots. This is an instinctual fear reaction, as a bird whose tail is touched by another animal could soon be a dead bird.

Selecting a Type of Parrot

More than 300 species of parrots are identified by their physical and behavioral similarities as well as by common native habitats. However, extreme variations can exist between individuals of the same species or subspecies, even among clutchmates (siblings). Generally, a smaller species is expected to present less-invasive habits, but this is not always so, as even small parrots may possess surprisingly "big" voices. For example, both Amazons and full-sized macaws are loud, but Ama-

zons are more likely to use their ear-splitting calls frequently. Several mid-sized and smaller species—including Quakers, Brotegeris, lories, and nanday and sun conures—are notorious for piercing, stubborn bluster.

It's impossible to predict exactly how each person in a particular household will react to a new parrot. However, by interviewing those who live and work closely with psittiformes, we can document how people respond to parrots. The table of Potential Issues by Species on page 7 is *not* a rating of the birds, but rather a collection of reported complications affecting *humans* who live with them. Hundreds of breeders, trainers, and regular parrot folk contributed their opinions about human ability to adjust to different species' space needs, mess generated, sound levels, and attention demands.

Species selection is discussed in greater detail in *Barron's Guide to*

Respect the rules of the establishment when shopping for a parrot. (scarlet macaw)

Companion Parrot Behavior and Parrots: A Complete Pet Owner's Manual, but responsible breeders and dealers will carefully describe both expected behaviors of species and behaviors particular to the bird being considered. After deciding what type of bird might work well in a particular environment, we will proceed to consider age.

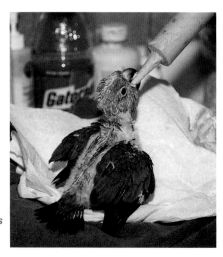

This neonatal jenday conure is being handfed with a syringe.

Transitions, Maturity, Perspective

It's easy to grab hold of the notion that a young parrot is less problematic than an older one but it ain't necessarily so. Raising a perfect parrot from weaning through adulthood is like trying to raise a perfect human. Baby parrots don't come with dispositional guarantees. If a parrot's personality is formed and unproblematic, especially if the species—perhaps an African grey, gallah, or other cockatoo—is known for developing vices or faults, then an older bird could be the most dependable choice. However, I would respect and carefully consider the bird's reputation. When buying an older Amazon, if the bird was said to bite people it "didn't like," I would be very, very careful during any interactions. Likewise, if a teenage cockatoo is said *not to be* a "screamer," then its habitual personality must have settled into predictable patterns, and the bird should be easily reinforced in non-screaming behaviors.

Parrot life stages can be described as:

Unweaned neonate. Many dependable sources encourage clients to place a deposit on recent hatchlings, then occasionally visit and play with their bird during the handfeeding period. That does not imply that we suggest taking an unweaned parrot home. Sensitive handling and periodic interactions during the handfeeding process can

Children and birds must interact with careful supervision in new and unfamiliar settings. (Meyer's parrot)

reduce the stress experienced when the youngster moves to the new home after fledging and weaning.

Fully weaned. For quite some time, this has been considered ideal. Now, many sensitive breeders also insist on keeping babies until they have flown, preferably with other birds, for at least a week or two. This facilitates the development of balance and coordination, and may prevent later development of feather-damaging behaviors or other unintended consequences. The presence of like companions allows fledglings to learn

bird-like ways necessary for success-ful life in a winged, feathered body.

Adolescent or juvenile. While many breeders and dealers don't like to keep parrots more than a few weeks past weaning, birds that have lingered longer can be some of the best finds in aviculture. Whether the bird stayed with the breeder or was returned from a first unsuccessful placement, it may have already over-come developmental phases that might have proved difficult in different hands. The immune system is closer to fully formed, minimizing the possi-

Larger birds might injure smaller birds during unsupervised play. (baby lovebirds and grey parrots)

bility of health issues; it's easier to see the personality at this age than in a younger bird. Smaller parrots, such as green cheeked conures (phyurras), Quakers, and budgies, may outgrow this phase quickly, perhaps by the end of the first year. Very large parrots might still be considered juvenile at three or four years old.

Sexual, but immature. Just as humans are capable of having babies before being able to provide for them, parrot pairs may lay fertile eggs before they are mature enough to raise them. Birds in this developmental stage are "practicing" behaviors necessary in the future: they may solicit sex, chew wood (almost compulsively), and regurgitate for favorite people, toys, or appliances. Unless health or behavioral issues were not resolved previously, a bird of this age is probably an excellent choice.

These baby Senegal parrots are being fed with a paper cup.

Potential Issues by Species

Group 1: Potential Issues are MINIMAL
Budgie (parakeet), lovebird, cockatiel, Bouke's parakeet, parrotlet
These birds have minimal needs and modest related costs. Most individuals and families can probably adjust to one of these birds.

Group 2: Potential Issues are AVERAGE
Quaker (monk parrot), small Poicephalus, Rosella, Pionus, ringneck, small conure, Brotegeris
These birds usually have reasonable, easy-to-accommodate needs that can be provided in most homes. A few individuals or individual members of a family may be intolerant of these birds.

Group 3: Potential Issues can be NUMEROUS
Large conures, mid-sized macaws, Cape, small cockatoos, caiques, lories, African greys, Amazons, eclectus
These birds are best accommodated in well-balanced families or by solitary individuals who know themselves to be tolerant and amenable. More than a few humans may be unable to adjust to these birds.

Group 4: Potential Issues can be EXTREME
Large macaws, large cockatoos, large Amazons, a few conures
These birds may require extreme, specialized accommodation and are suited to individuals who know themselves to be generous, consistent, and tolerant. Many people may be unable or unwilling to adjust to these birds.

Sexually mature. By the time a small parrot is two or a large one is ten, or somewhere in between, these very sexual creatures' behavior may be dominated by extreme pressure to breed. At this time, the bird will be searching for or defending nest sites, preventing access to favored territory, masturbating, and regurgitating on almost anything. Male birds, especially, might chew massive amounts of wood to toothpicks every day or might instinctively overeat, as a means of preparing for the difficult task of feeding babies. Watch for signs of egg binding in female birds.

Past breeding age. While a twenty-something Amazon or Umbrella cockatoo might not be what most people consider a "dream bird," a "retired breeder" can be an excellent human companion. Unless extreme territorialism, frantic calls for a mate, and compulsive toothpick-making were reinforced into habits, they can be easily left behind with enriched environment and positive reinforcement in a new or remodeled environment.

A human with an eclectic personality may be attracted to an eclectus parrot.

Elderly. Elderly parrots well past their breeding years might be the sweetest of all companion birds (or might not). They may require special perches, more sleep than a younger bird, and dietary accommodations such as milk thistle for liver support. While they may continue talking or even learn new words, extreme loud calls for mates may be distant, forgotten memories.

Look for clear, shining, lively eyes. (green-cheeked conure)

Selecting a Particular Bird

If talking is high on your list of priorities, look for a bird that is already talking. The bird's eyes should be clear, shining, and lively. Look for an alert, curious bird. Young parrots exhibiting notable aggression, extreme shyness, or fear should be avoided until these issues are resolved. Mature birds shown outside their familiar environment might be uncharacteristically nice. Mature birds shown in familiar or "claimed" territory might seem protective.

The beak should be symmetrical, nostrils and tongue dry. A hands-on physical examination should reveal that the edge of the keel bone is easily felt but not seen either as protruding past breast muscle or as "cleavage." Papillae lining the slit at the back of the throat inside the beak should be sharp and dry.

Feet should open and close and be well situated under the bird. A normal, healthy parrot naps or sleeps on only one foot with the other tucked up inside belly feathers. If this bird steps immediately onto a human hand, one foot is warmer than the other. Inspect the functioning of all eight toes. Look for eight toenails. One or two missing or malfunctioning toes or talons won't affect adjustment. Multiple toe or nail issues might require special accommodation.

Droppings should be well formed, with three observable parts: feces (solid material), urates (white "chalky" material), and liquid (clear fluid).

Runny droppings might suggest a health issue or could mean that the bird has recently eaten fruit. Veterinary examination is necessary to confirm the bird's health.

Don't be overly concerned about less-than-perfect feathers on a parrot under two years old. Baby psittiformes can be clumsy, especially if unaccustomed to trimmed wing feathers. Frayed and broken feathers are to be expected on active, playful youngsters. Juvenile birds may have ratty-looking, broken tail feathers until they learn preening and develop coordination. Ask your avian veterinarian to evaluate the health of any bird with multiple stress bars or damage lines straight across multiple fully formed and open feathers.

While most parrot species are not sexually dimorphic—without color differences or genitalia—behavioral differences can often be observed in individuals of opposite sexes. Now that sex can be safely and inexpensively determined with DNA testing, it's a good idea to find out immediately if your bird is a cock (male bird) or a hen (female bird). If a parrot is known to be female, then we can watch for signs of egg binding (a rare but potentially fatal occurrence) in the future. If the bird is male, we can work to compensate for "jealous" or territorial behavior that might develop with maturity.

Usually, we can expect males to be less cautious, more exploratory as juveniles, and more overtly sexual and territorial as adults. Hens may be shyer or quieter, or could be more

Look for an alert, curious bird. (male eclectus parrot)

overt and boisterous, but this is another place where nothing is cast in stone. Don't fall for the notion that a male bird will automatically be nicer, for although most hens do seem gentler and more cautious, we see many very gregarious, outgoing hens, even several struggling with very aggressive phases. One of the most beautiful and occasionally blood-

The Honeymoon Period

Like horses, mature, long-lived parrots are usually cautious when entering a new home. The first few days or weeks might be virtually problem-free as the bird studies the language, environment, and other members of the flock. During this time, wanted behaviors are usually easily stimulated, and unwanted behaviors can be just as easily ignored. Many parrots leave their behavior problems in the last home if they are not reinforced in a rich, exciting new environment.

When a parrot blissfully destroys wood, it may be demonstrating its nesting skills. (male Solomon Island eclectus)

thirsty parrots I have ever known was a female yellow-naped Amazon.

Look for sellers who are sensitive to their birds' needs. Some birds prefer people to birds; some like birds more than people. If the presence of other birds is important for a particular parrot, then that bird should be available only to a home with other birds.

A wise new parrot owner expects nothing more or less than a miniature dragon. (Moluccan cockatoo)

Likewise, if a parrot prefers people exclusively, it might be available only to a home with no other birds.

Expectations

One of the easiest ways to be set up for disappointment with a new parrot is to have expectations about who or what the new bird will be. Parrots have survived wild in spite of small sizes and bright colors by being intelligent and careful. Expect a smart, cautious animal that is intent on its own agenda—a whimsical individual who expects to do whatever it chooses to do, whenever it chooses to do so, and not, necessarily, to do what we want it to do. The bird will talk when it's darn good and ready, scream when it's darn good and ready, and might bite when anybody tries to "make" it do something it's not ready to do.

While a parrot can learn to be polite and tolerate almost anyone, no person or bird can be "made to" or "required" to "like" somebody. With a parrot, affection may develop spontaneously or may not. It might disappear if not nurtured and reinforced, or it might not.

When bringing a parrot into the home, expect nothing resembling a puppy. A wise family expects a flying miniature "dragon" with a can opener on its face. Like mythological dragons in so many ancient cultures, our parrots fly, and sometimes they can absolutely seem to "breathe a little fire."

Chapter Two
The Development of Behavior

An easy-to-live-with parrot is neither fearful nor aggressive, noisy nor quiet; enjoys spending time alone, but is ready to "rock and roll" when others seek interplay. In order to develop a balance of interaction and independence, cooperation and confidence, each feathered individual needs a different balance of attention and privacy. A parrot needs bird skills such as eating, climbing, flapping, chewing, and playing independently, in addition to cuddling.

During the period between fledging and sexual maturity, the juvenile parrot becomes an "information sponge." Coordination is fine-tuned for this flying athlete, enabling the progression of exploration and learning phases. A healthy young bird appears to have a compulsive desire to investigate every detail of every aspect of everything. The environment should be nursery-school-like— rich in color, sound, and appropriate opportunity. Limiting choices and experiences during this phase can affect the bird's intellectual and behavioral development.

The young parrot will be trying to copy behavior from anyone and everyone, especially "rivals," and will improvise whatever behavior seems to get the best, most interesting attention. If nobody demonstrates what to do, the bird might follow one of several predictable paths: take over, flip out, take over, chew up everything in reach, take over, scream when someone leaves the room, take over, chase customers out of the store, etc. The "take over" lane on this boulevard can be prominent and swift-moving in Quaker parrots and lories. This passion to control is often seen in companion cockatoos, yellow-headed Amazons (especially yellow napes), Poicephalus, and Caiques; but it might appear even in the tiniest parrot.

A well-socialized parrot will usually cooperate, walk or fly calmly from place to place, usually cooperate, chew appropriate accessories only, usually cooperate, talk softly whenever anybody walks by, usually cooperate, try to go home with customers, and, of course—if it's in the right mood—it will cooperate.

It's All About Payoff

Effective socialization involves reinforcing only behaviors we wish to see again, and "reinforcement" can be almost anything. The first form of reinforcement a bird encounters is comfort. Even before the egg hatches, parrot parents hear their babies and are stimulated to provide warmth and comfort for the developing embryo. If they don't hear a baby inside, they might choose to ignore the egg, and it won't hatch.

Upon hatching, the neonatal bird encounters food as a reward for vocalizing and competing with clutch mates to be fed. This new reward is reinforced by the familiar feelings of

An easy-to-live-with parrot enjoys playing alone, but is ready to "rock and roll" when others seek interplay. (military macaw)

comfort. Food remains a significant reinforcer throughout most parrots' lifetimes. A parrot also develops self-reward, that is, doing what feels good because it feels good. In a human, this would be like spending money, assembling a jigsaw puzzle, or playing golf.

Because parrots are highly social, interaction with other creatures also stimulates feelings of well-being. Almost any kind of interaction with humans—visual, vocal, or physical— might be perceived as a reward by an eager young bird. This might be problematic, however, as some youngsters love interaction so much that any action—even screaming or throwing plates against the wall— might be interpreted by the bird as a reward.

A companion parrot benefits greatly from access to many different opportunities for happily playing alone. Intermittent rewards can help to establish independent activities as routine, habitual. It is also important not to reinforce negative behaviors—such as stealing eyeglasses off of strangers' faces, biting, or screaming when somebody leaves the room—no matter how cute they seem the first time we see them.

Most early "beak on skin" activity is experimental. The youngster tries that soon-to-be-powerful beak and observes human responses to its use. It studies how much pressure can be exerted to generate a desired response. An incredible amount of "research" may be done on this process. When too much pressure is

Unintentional Reinforcement

Premium baby parrots don't usually come into the home biting. As a young bird acclimates, it becomes increasingly experimental, exploratory, and then territorial. This is noticeable as juvenile beaks grow both stronger and harder. Most young parrots appear delighted with the process and results of beak use. This might be troubling if the bird figures out that it enjoys watching humans jump and scream when its beak is applied to their flesh.

While consistent rewards can establish new behavior, intermittent rewards effectively reinforce known behaviors. Once a bird has been rewarded even once for an improvised behavior, that behavior will appear again and stands a good chance of becoming an established part of the bird's reper-tory. Often, after nips and bites have been accidentally reinforced, the birds themselves tell us the manner of unintentional reinforcement. For example, laughing when a bird uses its beak on flesh can produce a bird that nips or bites and then laughs.

The common occurrence of biting plus laughing demonstrates how very important the laughter of the favorite person is to companion parrots. Birds want to know that their companions are well. Laughter is also easier to deliver than food rewards. Unfortunately, it's also easy to accidentally laugh, thereby accidentally rewarding amusing but unwanted behavior. It also helps if everyone in the household learns to interact in ways that don't provoke the bird to bite.

exerted on skin, take care that the reaction is neither enjoyable nor provocative to the bird. If the response is "fun," the bite may occur again.

The best response to beak-on-skin activity is diverting the bird's attention—perhaps with a hand-held toy—or just putting the bird down. An interactive young parrot quickly learns cooperation if it wants to play. We can also reinforce any appropriate use of the beak. A parrot that learns it will get all the atten-tion it needs with sweet, sweet kisses, and will be most likely to use that beak sweetly and sensitively each time it touches skin.

The Effective Environment

An effective environment is the easiest, most natural way to a hap-pily adjusted bird.

As a well-planned environment is its own reward, height, cage, terri-

A curious young parrot appears to have a compulsive desire to investigate every detail of every aspect of everything it can reach. (cockatiel)

and their birds to understand each other, I have seen quite a few pleasant, charming, well-behaved parrots who had no training whatsoever. Their owners have—often intuitively—provided an environment that prevented the development of the "big three" problems—screaming, biting, and feather chewing.

Height

Whether the parrot looks up or down at a housemate can influence how the bird will interact with that person and can be instrumental in the development of territorialism. A normal parrot defending its home environment will usually be sweet, friendly, and cooperative with humans it looks up to and threatening or nippy toward any creature—man, woman, dog, or cat—upon whom it looks down.

This is often observed in public places where people are allowed to handle large parrots. It is not coincidental that a pet shop with waist-high perches has more interactive birds than a shop housing them above eye level.

Height can also sometimes compensate for fearfulness in companion birds. Startling behavioral changes have been brought about by either lowering "mean" birds or raising "shy" ones.

Cage/Space

A bird needs a spacious, easy-to-climb cage. I see a correlation between the amount of space a parrot occupies and the ferocity with

tory, location, light, accessories, and access to appropriate choices have undeniable influence on the development of acceptable behaviors. Manipulating these elements can usually prevent and sometimes correct common behavior problems.

While training is important, I believe environment may have greater influence on behavioral adjustment in companion parrots. Even a well-trained hookbill may develop serious behavior problems if denied an adequate environment. During many years of helping people

which it seeks to control that space. The influence of space on behavior is particularly observable in the case of African greys and macaws, either of which can be unfavorably affected by a poorly planned environment. I disagree completely with avian writers who say that macaws make poor pets after the age of two, nor do I feel that macaws require any more "training" than an Amazon or grey parrot. In the presence of a well-reinforced step-up response, good conditioning to restraint, cooperation for flapping exercises, and aggression-prevention strategies by human companions, I believe that a macaw in a well-planned environment requires no more time or attention than, for example, a yellow nape. On the other hand, a macaw requires considerably more *environment* than an Amazon.

I think a bird needs a cage at least one and a half times its untrimmed wing span in at least two, but preferably, three dimensions. That is, if the bird has a 2-foot (.6-m) wing span, the cage where the bird spends the majority of its time needs to be at least 3 feet (1 m) tall, 3 feet (1 m) wide, and 3 feet (1 m) deep.

If space is marginal or barely adequate, behavior might be enhanced by manipulating the bird's perception of space. For example, it is not a good idea to take an established companion bird from a larger cage and place it directly into a permanent smaller cage. If a lifestyle change dictates that the bird must go to a smaller cage, it is best kept in an

A healthy young parrot will appear quite delighted with the process and results of beak use. (hyacinth macaw)

even smaller cage for a few weeks, then introduced to the new cage, which will now seem larger.

One of my favorite examples of manipulation of perceived space is a piece of Chris Davis advice from years ago. It seems that a particular bird would scream "all the time" if it was not allowed to sit on top of its cage. The owner was unable to allow the bird that much liberty, so Chris recommended a cage within a much larger cage. The bird could sit on top of the inner cage yet remain restrained; presumably the bird would have the feeling of being outside "the" cage and would, therefore, scream less.

Territory

Spending too much time in one place can contribute to the development of territorialism. Monitor and modify this with a well-planned captive environment, including a "roost" and multiple "foraging" areas. In the wild, most parrots sleep in approximately the same place every night (unless they are actually nesting). Every day they forage in several areas where there might be a newly maturing food source; a past-its-prime field to be scoured for leftovers; a known dependable source of minerals or insects; a shallow pool for bathing; a cool, shady place for an afternoon nap; or a couple of potential new haunts for investigation.

A "home bird" forced to remain in exactly the same place day after day may come to guard that space so aggressively that no one can service the cage or even walk by without a feigned, attempted, or successful attack. The provision of multiple "foraging" areas within the home can minimize this behavior by enlarging perceived "territory." One might provide several fixed-location birdproof areas or one portable play area to be moved from room to room. A bird who enjoys multiple play or foraging areas requires less sleeping cage space than a bird who remains in or on the cage most of the time. For optimal result, the sleeping cage is placed far from foraging areas.

Just as a bird spending too much time in one place becomes possessively defensive of that territory, a bird that spends too much time with one human possessively defends that "human territory." Occasional visits outside the home, particularly with less-than-favorite humans, lessen the ill effects of immoderate bonds to perceived territory, including "human territory." Since a young bird may bond—at least initially—to a favorite human in a territorial manner, excursions out of the home with less-than-favorite humans will support a balanced relationship between the companion bird and all humans in the home (the flock).

Location

In addition to the influences of height, space, and territory, the location of a companion parrot's space plays a role in social adjustment. Common and predictable screaming behaviors can easily be stimulated by actual or perceived isolation from "the flock" or the flock's activities. Perceived isolation might be something as simple as helping the bird to see people as they come around a corner (add a mirror, possibly one of those convex "shoplifter" mirrors) or inability to see what everyone else is watching (be sure the bird can see the television, or it might go crazy trying to figure out what everyone is watching). Of course, actual isolation in a basement or back room is the worst possible thing to do to a bird screaming for attention.

I also see biting behaviors in quite a few birds who must be frequently rushed past because of a cage located in the eye of what might be a daily "hurricane"—the fixing of breakfast and hustling children off to school or the home-protection efforts of a couple of boisterous dogs. Sometimes moving a cage only a few feet can minimize this effect. For example, a bird area that must, because of space limitations, be on either side of a busy doorway might elicit better bird behavior on one side of the doorway rather than the other. Behavioral benefits from the move might be seen because people or dogs customarily rush in what is now a relatively different direction or because the bird has better near vision on one side than the other.

A well-designed companion parrot environment includes many textures and shapes for the bird to explore. (Jardine's parrot)

down on the bird like rainfall rather than being directed at any part of the bird's anatomy. A bird that is responding to rainfall, either by cheerfully bathing or merely tolerating the water, will not be engaging in unwanted behavior.

Rainfall

Even "rainfall" is an important part of the indoor environment. A bird that enjoys frequent showers is less prone to aggression, roaming, screaming, or other behaviors related to unexpressed energy.

This differs from squirting as punishment in that it is administered carefully in a manner resembling rainfall *before* unwanted behavior occurs. The source of the spray, usually a spray bottle, is held lower than the bird's head and far enough away from the bird that the bird is not focused on the tool providing the spray mist. The spray mist is aimed over the bird's head so that it falls

"Daylight"

When evaluating a particular bird's environment, attention must be paid to the quality and amount of light the bird receives. Required amount of full spectrum light and length of daylight periods probably vary with each type of bird. A bird receiving too little light or low-quality light may be poorly feathered, inactive, overweight, and may fail to vocalize. This is sometimes accompanied by low thyroid output, which may or may not be coincidental. An outdoor cage situated to provide for and protect from direct sunlight contributes to both good health and good behavior.

A bird receiving too much light might exhibit hypersexuality, irritability, screaming, biting, and feather chewing. A person seeking to normalize a particular bird's environment might investigate light periods in the bird's native range, altering the length of indoor "daylight" for behavioral effect. Light periods may be manipulated to stimulate or terminate breeding, to modify lethargy, obesity, hypersexuality, aggression, screaming, self-mutilation, and failure to talk.

Accessories

No well-designed indoor parrot environment is complete without an evaluation of accessories—chewing, ringing, holding, climbing, swinging, preening, and "bopping" toys, and perches. The easiest, least expensive, and most accessible accessories are tree branches with bark. Branches with bark help keep beak and toenails appropriately worn and help prevent foot problems and related behavioral issues. I like ailanthus or sumac branches. Loro Parque in the Canary Islands provides fresh pine branches weekly. I think most taller trees are probably safe. I consider all shrubs, fruit trees, and trees that might have been sprayed with chemicals to be potentially harmful. Clean and examine branches for bugs and fungus.

Every bird should have several choices of commonly favored activities, such as ringing a bell, preening a fuzzy pseudo-friend, climbing both fixed and swinging objects, and "bopping" a fleeting, shiny reflection. Sometimes a particular toy might hang in the cage for quite some time before the bird learns how to play with it. Sometimes a toy will be ignored for long periods only to be discovered as a favorite buddy. A well-rounded hookbill should probably have at least a half dozen toys, some of which are routinely withheld and returned to reinforce good behavior or distract from anticipated bad behavior.

Many active, well-behaved, kind-to-humans parrots have daily play rituals that involve "beating up" or otherwise physically dominating a toy. Just because a bird abuses a toy doesn't mean that it will abuse humans. In fact, like frequent drenching showers, abuse of toys releases energy that might otherwise emerge as aggression against humans.

Choice and Confidence

Especially during periods of rapid learning, the bird should have access to many appropriate choices. Selecting from alternatives provides intellectual stimulation and confidence-building experience, enabling the bird to compensate for its naturally cautious nature. A properly weaned young parrot comes with a taste for a variety of foods. Try not to reduce or limit the number of choices of foods offered, although quantities must be limited to prevent eating only favored foods. Now is the best time to encourage the bird to make other types of decisions, as well.

A young parrot must have appropriate options about how and where it spends its time, and numerous toys with which to play. Even if a bird chooses not to play on a small second perch joined to its main play area by a rope, or decides not to play with a particular toy, the presence of the second toy or play area has provided an opportunity for "successful" decision making. This supports the development of curiosity and confidence, encouraging the bird to explore the alternatives of an ever-changing world.

Sometimes it seems that the young parrot is trying to learn everything we are trying to keep it from learning. It is trying to learn absolutely everything. For this reason and for safety, the bird should have access only to appropriate choices. If unwanted behavior isn't improvised, it cannot be inadvertently reinforced. In other words, the cage should not be positioned beside a shelf of valuable miniatures or an expensive picture frame, but rather, it should hold bird toys and/or parrot-chewable "art" (a bird toy, of course).

In an inadequately-designed environment, a parrot might find lots of unacceptable things to do. Such a bird might learn to "act up" for attention. Although it's counterintuitive, the best course of action when confronted by a bird behaving badly is to suggest good behavior by saying "Be a good bird!" This can distract the bird from continuing unwanted behavior and might be coupled with a suggestion of appropriate behavior.

For better or worse, human responses usually—often unintentionally—reinforce companion parrot behavior. (Jardine's parrot)

People are the most influential part of the companion parrot's environment as they stimulate, provoke, and reinforce the bird's behavior, as well as provide for the physical elements of the environment. The ability to modify a companion bird's behavior is dependent upon the willingness of humans to modify their own behavior or to accommodate changes required to stimulate new behaviors in the bird.

Humans often constitute the only "flock" after which the bird can pattern its behavior. Under the influence of an angry—even a passively angry—owner, a bird can learn "violent" behavior. If humans in the environment taunt or ignore the bird, if they taunt or ignore each other, a companion parrot can easily develop

The Lifeguard Principle

It seems easier to tell someone what *not to do* than to effectively, successfully suggest what to do. But "no" might not be the most effective path. A "No smoking" sign reminds some people that they'd like a smoke, a "No running" sign reminds a happy child that it's fun to run. Modern behavior managers now advocate saying what you want to see rather than what you don't. Lifeguards are advised to say, "*Slow down* or get in the pool."

This is probably more difficult than it sounds. "No, don't bite" feels so much more spontaneous, but saying the word "bite" can stimulate, suggest, or reinforce the behavior. Naming a behavior does suggest that behavior, and does, for better or worse, stimulate the

desire to do it. This is especially true of parrots. A bird told that it is a "good bird" or a "pretty bird" is stimulated to engage in behaviors that it associates with those familiar, welcome words.

"Be careful" can also distract from unwanted behavior in this way: whenever you see that the bird is going to fall, about to drop something, or experience some other unwanted event, say, "Be careful." The words "be careful" become a termination stimulus. The bird will learn to stop, evaluate the situation, then continue or change tasks. Eventually, if you see that a bird is about to bite, the words, "Be careful" can distract from the unwanted behavior and redirect the bird's energy.

undesirable or antisocial behaviors. It is not unusual for owners of a good talking type of bird that is not talking to admit that humans do not talk to each other in their home.

Even the most social individual enjoys occasional solitude. While a confident bird should be patterned to step up from inside the cage, this is not always feasible with shyer birds. I believe companion parrots benefit from having the opportunity to choose to come out of the cage or not. A shy or fearful bird should especially not be required to come out for non-

emergency interactions if it chooses not to do so. Just open the cage door. Most confident, well-accommodated birds climb to the top of the door or to the top of the cage and can be picked up there. If it doesn't come out, if it's eating or playing or simply doesn't want to come out, step away and come back later. Just be sure the bird does come out of the cage from time to time, even if that means sometimes feeding it outside the cage.

As with human teenagers, unless a bird is acclimated to accept

Toys made from food can help a young bird develop a taste for variety. (severe macaw)

change, anything unfamiliar might be resisted, avoided, or feared. If, however, the bird has learned to experience and explore, its ongoing behavior can often be maintained merely by manipulating the environment.

Face-to-Face, Side-by-Side

A young parrot can easily learn to expect constant face-to-face attention with humans. When we're talking directly to the bird, one-on-one, when we're holding or petting it, we can do nothing else. Our attention is held captive. Cockatoos and African greys are especially prone to this, but any human-bonded parrot can become virtually addicted to attention.

Quality social time with a companion parrot also means sharing side-by-side activities such as eating, bathing, talking, singing, exercising, and expressing affection with other humans in the presence of the bird. The bird learns autonomous behavior by seeing it and copying it. This leads to the development of independence. Extreme *independence*, where little or no interaction with humans is necessary, is easily achieved in many

A companion parrot might insist on face-to-face attention. (yellow-naped Amazon)

budgies, ringnecks, grass parakeets, Poicephalus, loric, and cockatiels. Extreme *dependence* can develop easily in cockatoos, African greys, eclectus, macaws, and almost any handfed parrot that is reinforced in dependence to the exclusion of independence, exploration, and curiosity.

Hands off, indirect social activities also facilitate bonding with a shy or cautious bird. Even if it doesn't enjoy being handled, a parrot still has a compelling need to spend time with a social group. I have seen many difficult-to-correct behavioral problems develop in birds that are not allowed to see the human "flock" eat and birds that cannot, because of their location, see what humans are watching (usually the television).

Communication

Even while still inside the egg, a baby parrot verbally communicates its need for parents to provide food and care. Failure to do so, especially just after hatching, results in death by neglect—swift elimination of non-verbal babies from the gene pool. This natural selection process ensures an adult individual adept at finding its mate and flock when separated, communicating safety, alarm, and an unknown number of other messages to its peers.

Although much remains to be learned about why, how, and what parrots communicate verbally, we know that their ability to verbalize is not limited to communication in their

own language—that they can and do learn other animal languages as well as human language. Studies done by Dr. Irene Pepperberg with African grey parrots are particularly startling, revealing even an ability to understand numbers, including the concept of zero.

Birds spend a large portion of their lives scolding, chattering, and singing to each other. They bill and coo, scream and curse. They are particularly vocal in territorial disputes, but even when comfortable in their own space, they are famous for generating great volumes of sound (some people even call it noise). They are most likely to try to communicate verbally when separated from their "flock"—when they can hear, but not see their companions. To establish a verbally interactive human/avian relationship, begin by trying to understand and responding to the bird's sounds.

Speak the bird's language: When spending time with a "prespeech" bird, you will begin to notice redundant sounds associated with particular events. An African grey may "click" when it sees a favorite toy. A budgie or Amazon may "trill" to the hair dryer or "tut, tut, tut, tut" to the reflection in the mirror. If you can reproduce the situation by making the same sound as the bird, then enticing the bird to repeat the sound, you have made a major communication breakthrough. You have modeled a behavior for the bird, then stimulated the bird to mimic the behavior.

Tell stories: A companion parrot loves to be entertained—particularly

if it hears its own name repeated in a story. "Once upon a time, there was a pudgy, green Amazon named Portia. One day, when Portia was only a naked nestling, he fell from the tree where his mother had laid him . . . ."

It may not really matter what words come between the "Portia's," but a steady stream of words in a friendly tone, freely interspersed with the bird's name, will capture its curiosity and establish direct, personal communication.

Be redundant: A companion parrot will usually pick up the word it hears most frequently, usually, a greeting. "Hello" in English might be difficult for some birds, so try the Spanish greeting, "Hola" (pronounced "Oh la"), or the more continental "Ciao" (pronounced "Chow"). Birds usually repeat single-syllable greetings first—"What," "Hi," "Ciao,"—followed later by "Hello" and "What 'cha doin'?"

Quality social time with a parrot should include sharing side-by-side activities. (black-headed caique)

A parrot might pick up the sounds of human infants or children before learning to say true words. (yellow-naped Amazon)

He appeared frustrated that whoever was ringing that bell would not respond to him! Unlike a dog barking at a dog on television—a natural response in the dog's own language—Portia was making a learned response to a stimulus and making that response with learned sounds, to him a "foreign" language.

Be conversant: While some parrots merely repeat individual words, others repeat whole or partial conversations, and they do so at surprisingly appropriate moments. They may say "Hi," pause for response, then "Whatcha doin'?" when you come home; "Bye," pause, and "Take it easy," when you leave; "Come here" when they want you to come over; "What!" when frightened; and "Night, Night!" when it's time for bed.

Set a talkative example: A young parrot that is not talked to or spends all its time with birds or humans who don't talk to each other will have less desire to communicate verbally.

Baby babble: Baby parrots usually get the cadence down first. They may mutter unrecognizable syllables and practice babbling for hours, sometimes quietly and sometimes loudly before actually producing understandable words.

The riff (or roll): Every day, healthy, talking parrots spend a noticeable amount of time repeating what seems like their full repertoire of words. If a word disappears from its usual position in the sequence, it may not be heard again. Usually, however, the word will reappear later. In the instance of very intelli-

After the greeting, the next most frequently repeated word in the household is often the name of a child or another pet. Amazons are famous for making everybody crazy by calling children or other pets in the mother's voice. Birds love "itty" sounds, like "pretty bird" and "itty, bitty, pretty one." A large number of talking companion parrots say "Here, Kitty, Kitty, Kitty."

Portia, my yellow-naped Amazon, greets the doorbell with "Hello" and answers a knock with "Come in." I once encountered him repeating "Hello" in a strange, almost frantic manner. First he said "Hello" in his greeting voice, then "Hello?" questioningly, then "Hello! Hello!" angrily. He then repeated the sequence. Upon investigation, I found him watching a TV game show that included a bell similar to my doorbell.

gent species, I believe the dropped word does not require daily use but is learned sufficiently to be called forth when the occasion arises.

Cooing: Soothing "OOOOO" sounds can be helpful when wishing to calm an angry, upset, or frightened bird. Totally wild or totally tame, all our feathered friends love lots of "Pooor, baaby" and "Pooor, pooor birdie."

Singing: Whether you want your bird's undivided attention or wish to express joy to your bird, nothing is quite as effective as song. Many a parrot can be something like mesmerized by singing humans, and other parrots will court or sing along. Even if you are just "hanging out" with the bird, it will appreciate your song just as much as you enjoy the bird's song. I do not usually recommend some Amazons to voice students, as these birds can aggressively interfere with practice.

Whispering: Sometimes, particularly in dealing with a screamer, the most effective way to get the bird's attention is by whispering. This behavior communicates to the bird that its screams have been heard. If you cannot understand why it is screaming or are unable to change whatever it's screaming about, at least you are modeling an appropriate method of getting attention. If the bird is a "quick study," it might catch on and try whispering for your attention now or later.

To whistle or not to whistle: Some people contend that if one teaches a good-talking bird to whistle,

it will not reach its full talking potential. Because a bird has no vocal cords, speech is accomplished by "moving" the lining of the bifurcated trachea into different configurations while expelling air across those openings. Therefore, a talking parrot is actually "whistling" in syllables, and true whistling is more natural and easier to accomplish than talking. Types of parrots with a propensity for mimicking appear to have good control over the musculature in the trachea. Types of parrots with poor talking potential may have an inefficiently shaped trachea or poor control over the muscles of the trachea.

A very good talker might occasionally become so enchanted with a new whistle that it will discontinue talking in favor of whistling for a time. It happened to my young yellow nape when a well-meaning friend taught him to wolf whistle. Portia didn't talk for a couple of weeks, and nearly

Whistling can be a gateway to other vocalizations or might wind up being a parrot's preferred "language." (Jardine's parrot)

drove me mad with that obnoxious whistle.

I don't think it's a bad idea, however, to use whistling as a substitute or a transition for teaching birds who find talking difficult or for birds, such as the female cockatiel, in whom speech is considered very difficult. Many parrots that may be only fair talkers can become accomplished whistlers. I know quite a few who loudly entertain with "London Bridge," "Colonel Bogie March," or "Beethoven's Fifth" at any opportunity.

Don't scream: It is very easy to teach most parrots to scream. This is an instinctive reaction to visual isolation and barrier frustration and is easily reinforced by screaming back and forth from one room to another. Also, no matter how loudly a bird screams—particularly if it is a good talker—don't try to reprimand it by screaming back. You might be teaching another loud call to practice at sunrise. Better to deliver a stern look and a forceful reprimand in a calm, assertive voice followed by some form of distraction (exercise, bathing, or toys).

Use words in context/avoid recordings: If you want a bird to merely mimic, a recording might be the most effective way to accomplish that objective. I believe, however, that the potential for damage is greater than the perceived benefits. Having to listen to the same 20 seconds of material over and over can stress the bird and contribute to screaming, unexplained aggression, self-mutilation, or intellectual withdrawal.

In contrast, a bird taught to use words in context is more likely to use them at appropriate times in appropriate situations. Can you imagine being taught to make sounds that don't mean anything? I believe that using words the bird can say to represent their meaning enhances and stimulates the bird's motivation to speak.

Don't talk dirty: Responsible owners understand that their parrots will outlive them, and they avoid teaching profanity. A bird with a dirty mouth might have a hard time finding a home when you're gone. Of course, they always seem to pick up just what we don't want them to say! The children of the widow on my block found out about Mom's new boyfriend when the budgie started saying, "Kiss me quick behind the door!"

Don't become discouraged if it seems to take a long time for the bird to learn to speak your language. It is an awesome accomplishment for any creature. I have seen birds who never managed a single word speak up to 20 words four years after their introduction to the home.

It is a parrot's nature to communicate verbally. Even if your bird is not fluent in your language, keep listening. I'm sure it is trying to tell you something.

The Good, the Bad, and the Over-bonded

Following cycles of exploratory behavior, we will see the beginnings of the development of a protective attitude toward territory, both actual territory and human "territory." This protective or territorial behavior might be related to a place, such as the dining room or kitchen counter, or it might be related to a situation, such as height. It might be related to nearness to humans, such as the back of the sofa, or it might be part of the favorite person, such as the shoulder or lap. Aggression can develop if the bird is allowed to establish territory on the human shoulder. Any parrot that will not immediately and peacefully comply with a step-up prompt from the shoulder can severely damage human eyes, ears, or lips. The baby parrot needs to know that you are a loving benefactor, not "territory" to be defended.

A parrot might decide that a reflective surface is either a mate or a rival, leading to many courtships with toasters and wars with hair dryers. A sexually mature parrot might decide that no one is allowed in the kitchen. A bird that has fixated on an object or territory must be denied access to them, if possible. An attacking bird might be picked up using a hand-held perch, a towel, or distraction devices and placed with an appropriate "surrogate enemy" toy. Parrots have a tremendous amount of energy. Indoors, that energy often comes out when expressing territorialism. This warlike, defensive, or hostile energy, must be expressed somehow; it is best expressed against a toy. Instinctual territorialism can be manipulated by moving the bird's cage occasion-

A parrot at liberty in the home might take up residence in the kitchen and allow no others there. (potbellied pig and sulphur crested cockatoo)

ally, rearranging and changing toys periodically, and guiding the bird to maintain interactions with more than one person.

Cooperation patterning such as step-ups are helpful in overcoming territorialism as we train the bird to be transported by humans from one place to another. The bird should have at least two regular areas in which to spend time: a roost (cage) in which to sleep and one or more foraging area(s). The bird should be dependent upon humans to get from one area to another by stepping onto the hand to get from the cage to the perch or shower every day. This "transportation dependence" helps the bird to understand that successful interactions with humans are rewarded with interesting, exciting things to do.

Few parrots can be trusted to stay peacefully on opposite shoulders of the same person at the same time. (Yellow-headed Amazon and green winged macaw)

A bird might prefer one person over another. A young bird expressing aggression against a less-favored person might change loyalties as more-adult behavior develops and begin attacking the previously-favored person. Bond switches and periodically changing loyalties are reported in African greys, cockatoos, Amazons, and conures; but I believe there is potential for this behavior in any parrot that is allowed to bite or chomp all but the favorite person. Occasional outings where the bird is handled by sensitive, astute, less-than-favorite humans can be used to manipulate bonding behaviors, improve patterning, and reduce territorialism.

The bird should interact with both "regulars" and "strangers." A companion parrot should attend as many human gatherings as safely possi-

ble. If the bird expresses dislike for one person, and these responses are not related to signals or body language from that person, then efforts must be made to improve the relationship with that person. This is not usually true "dislike" of a person, but rather an expression of territorial instinct that drives the bird to try to drive all but its favorites away.

As Time Goes By

In human infants, periods of fussiness can accompany transitions or precede great leaps in learning, such as when a baby learns to crawl over and reach a toy rather than scream for someone to deliver it. Likewise, juvenile parrots on the verge of making great learning strides can go through periods of fussiness just before making some sort of progress. Any parrot with trimmed wings might get a little noisy before finally figuring out how to say "commere" or grow enough feathers to fly across the room. A young bird may be irritable when growing new feathers, especially wing feathers. Detour around these behaviors or ignore them.

An unweaned or under-six-month-old parrot that is already threatening and biting people and/or objects other than toys must be given sound behavioral guidance immediately, as this can be a sign of serious problems developing. Aggression in an unweaned or newly-weaned bird can be easily reinforced as the bird's per-

sonality is being formed. If aggression is reinforced, it will escalate. Don't be shy if you think you might need professional assistance. A parrot behavior consultant is a lot like a dog trainer or horse trainer, and almost everyone who has had a horse or a dog has used the services of a trainer at one time or another.

A young parrot might also go through shy or fearful phases. Avoid stimulating repeated fear reactions. Transitional fearfulness may be a specific response to one person. If that is the case, try to figure out what stimulated the first enactment of the response and be careful not to repeat that interaction.

By two to three years of age, most parrots will be actively and frequently chewing anything chewable within reach. We will see a transition from a time when toys were hardly scratched, through a time when they are dismantled into parts, to a time when they are completely demolished into splinters. As these behaviors develop, it's necessary to increase the number and frequency of chewables in the restricted environments of both the cage and the play area.

As with human children, new behaviors can seem to appear from nowhere. For months, the bird will leave the picture frame behind the cage alone. Then one day, the picture frame is splintered on two sides. For years, the bird might put nothing into the water, then one day it will begin filling the water bowl with debris. A maturing parrot might suddenly begin pulling newspaper up through the grate. These behaviors are probably part of the parrot's instinctive drive to reproduce. The

If a parrot has not been socialized for interaction with humans by the time it is sexually mature, its instincts to reproduce might defeat training at that time. (blue and gold macaw)

human/avian interaction and to suppress or minimize breeding-related behaviors.

As breeding seasons approach, we will see heightened exploration, physical and emotional experimentation. The bird might even change loyalties, becoming aggressive around a newly-selected territory or a new favorite human (mate substitute). If a parrot has been allowed to over-bond to one human in the past, at this time, the formerly favorite human might be dumped for a more easily dominated companion. We must be ever vigilant to ensure that the bird is not excessively defensive of the territory around any human so that previous and predictable loyalties will not be abandoned.

Be sure to continue interacting with the maturing companion parrot—whenever it's in the right mood—in order to maintain tameness. Some birds will be easily kept tame; some will be difficult. Every bird will be a little different, with vast differences between species and between successfully socialized and unsocialized birds of the same type. Generally, the more consistent we are in all interactions, the more predictable the bird will be.

It might be necessary to take a feisty young parrot out of its familiar territory for at least a few days each year in order to repattern the bird and to reinforce interactions with unfamiliar humans. Vacations and indoor "outings" (visits to unfamiliar territory) may be beneficial at this time. Even a simple car ride with the

bird is doing what it was "programmed" to do. We must provide other appropriate things to chew and reinforce the bird for chewing appropriately.

Running Wild

Unlike dogs and cats that are spayed and/or neutered for behavioral reasons, companion parrots are allowed the full influence of their reproductive urges. A parrot expressing this natural instinct might chew the stereo speakers to splinters, decide to allow no one near the breakfast nook, regurgitate on your slippers, or masturbate on the dog. As with humans, instead of surgically altering the animal, we must learn to stimulate and reinforce different behavior. Techniques discussed here are intended to enhance favorable behaviors for

bird in a carrier can make a wonderful difference in a parrot's disposition. Sturdy carriers, careful transporting, seat belts, and meticulous wing feather trims will help to ensure safety on these outings.

At home the maturing parrot may become increasingly concerned with control issues, especially immediate environmental control. The bird might decide to defend a height territory, sofa, or floor territory. The bird might start attacking toes or tissues, or people sneezing or blowing their noses into tissues. A maturing parrot might also attack anyone cleaning with quick motions with paper towels. Remove the bird from the area before cleaning so that these behaviors are not reinforced.

A maturing parrot allowed a great deal of liberty in the home might become hyper-vigilant or aggressive around a suddenly and mysteriously selected territory. Expect heightened reactions to mirrors, shiny objects, and small appliances. The bird might attack the vacuum cleaner or hair dryer. The bird will be seeking both companions and interlopers in its reflections. At this time the bird might fixate strongly on an inanimate object, treating it either as a potential mate or an enemy to be attacked.

Even solitary parrots can develop sexual behaviors. Although many companion parrots limit "sexual" behaviors to courtship behaviors, including chewing, eating, and feeding, many birds will more overtly seek gratification. Expect to see masturbation in many healthy male

The Surrogate Enemy

Companion parrot behavior appears to benefit from the presence of at least one "enemy" to be regularly thwarted. The bird must select or identify this surrogate enemy from available options. Most do this spontaneously. Of course, it's important for this enemy not to be a living creature or a treasured possession, so several potential approved surrogate enemies must be provided. Unbreakable hanging toys or safe bells are excellent candidates for this parrot-selected "rival." If a companion parrot has no opportunity to release natural aggressive energy against an approved surrogate enemy when the instinct to do so is aroused, the bird is likely to direct that energy against whatever or whoever is closest.

birds and some female birds. A companion parrot might solicit copulation from a favorite human or engage in masturbation, masturbation display, or anxiety behaviors that sometimes include sexual gestures. Each bird's masturbation process is accompanied by that species' characteristic sounds, which an astute owner learns to recognize. My own hen cockatiel Pearl, who characteristically used only one note most of the time, whistled a male cockatiel song as she masturbated, in the corner of her cage.

Sexual behaviors should be ignored, as they can be accompanied by aggression or feather picking. A habitually masturbating companion bird may later choose those behaviors over mating even if a mate is offered. If the behaviors receive no payoff, they're less likely to reappear. However, since self-gratification is the very definition of self-rewarding behavior, a parrot might continue sexual behaviors regardless of whether or not they have been reinforced.

If the bird is either whacking or attacking a toy, leave it alone. It'll be seeking your attention soon enough. Then, even a mature bird can be patterned to cooperate. The more successful interactive experiences the young bird enjoys, the more it is reinforced in cooperation, the more likely interactive behavior will remain.

If a large parrot has not been socialized by the teen years, the bird's instincts to reproduce, along with the habitual self-rewarding behaviors that have developed, can challenge or defeat efforts to train the bird. During the teen years a parrot might develop both predictable and unpredictable biting behavior, especially in the perceived territory. Usually there will be plenty of warning: hyper-vigilance, eye movement, wing or tail display, charging with beak open, or any other body language that usually accompanies aggression in a particular individual.

The best way to deal with aggression in a sexually mature companion parrot is to avoid it. Do anything necessary to stimulate different behavior. Never allow the bird to chase or

harass people or animals. Just clap your hands for attention, say "Be a good bird," then return the bird to the cage in the calmest possible way. A bird being prompted to step up might be distracted with a toy or other inanimate object when threatening a bite while being prompted to step up.

Long-term Adjustment

Nutritious diet, safety, trust-building interactions, and ongoing environmental stimulation are important parts of life quality for a companion parrot. Companion human life-quality is equally as important, since humans control the environment for both. Just as parrots deserve a sense of well-being, the people who live with them have a right to enjoy their homes free from parrot attacks, temper tantrums, or screaming bouts.

However, nobody's perfect, and neither is any parrot. Nobody gets along with every life companion every single day, year after year. As time passes, the term "parrot stew" may sound occasionally tempting. New behaviors will develop, replacing old behaviors that might reappear at any moment or fade away forever. New social and emotional bonds will appear and old bonds may be broken. A parrot is an undomesticated, self-motivated animal. Companion humans must refrain from taking parrotlike behavior personally. If a parrot screams or nips or bites, consider the fact that it's trying to communicate, not simply punish. Again, acceptance and unconditional love are the paths to happiness here.

Chapter Three
Early Behavior Management

Just as humans may either continue to learn and explore as time and age pass—or else shut down, put on blinders, and never leave the house—companion parrots can follow different behavioral paths depending upon their day-to-day habits. If all the needs of humans and parrots in the home are being met—physically and behaviorally— then peace, comfort, and cooperation will result. If something is missing, or if something is "too much" for a particular individual, then the human/parrot relationship will be tested.

The Work of Play*

The life of a wild lovebird is probably no picnic. Wild birds must find food and water daily; select, court, and defend mates; compete for, prepare, and protect nest sites; lay and incubate eggs; nurture offspring, then teach them survival skills. They must compete with humans and all other animals for

---
*With Dianalee Deter

habitat while maintaining communication and relationships with other lovebirds—with time left over for preening and grooming.

A wild parrot is never bored. Essential survival tasks allow little "spare" time and that is filled with mate and flock social interactions. Humans may have to teach the parrot how to play, and many humans are simply too busy to play. A companion parrot needs indoor-acceptable activities to fill the hours and minutes of the days just as survival activities would fill its outdoor life. A lovebird that doesn't know how to play alone can be a very demanding lovebird. Fortunately, lovebirds very easily develop independent self-rewarding behaviors (toy play).

It would be great if we could just give a bird a toy and say, "Here, play with this," as we would with a child.

Many parrots might ignore or fear toys if they haven't learned the benefits of chewing, banging, and shredding the objects in the cage. Given a rich, stimulating assortment of toys, young parrots quickly develop and easily retain indepen-

Even very small parrots like this budgie can gain trust and confidence by observing and mimicking passive, nontactile interactions, including eye, beak (lip), and/or tongue movements.

it seems to belong to a favorite human, it might prove irresistible, even to a bird with a reputation for not playing with toys.

"**Keep away**" is good for piquing a parrot's interest in a new toy or food. Show the bird the toy or food only very briefly, at first. The bird is allowed to see the toy only long enough to become frightened of it. Then the favorite human can show excitement over having the toy and begin playing with it.

If a toy can be shredded, the person should shred it a bit. If it can be eaten, the person should eat some, while the bird watches. Show the object to the bird again. Give it to a rival. Show it to the bird again. Play with it again. Eventually the bird will lean closer and closer. By the time the bird is given the object, it will be excited to have it. Most birds succumb to curiosity within minutes. Some may take more than one session of this little game. Toys can simply lay around the environment and then can be gradually moved closer to the bird. Toys hung on the outside of the cage that have parts that can be pulled inside can be especially appealing.

Once a bird has seen many new toys, it will welcome new additions. Then comes the challenge of finding a toy that survives more than a few minutes. Some birds prefer objects that are not colorful. Shredded paper, twigs, natural rope, or vegetable-tanned leather may be more interesting than expensive toys. Newspaper pompoms can be irresistible to some

dent behaviors. Actually, independence probably comes more naturally than interaction.

If play behaviors don't develop in a young bird, they might not develop in that bird at all. A cautious parrot might need special encouragement from its owner. The following suggestions are usually all that is necessary to generate play behaviors in a young, healthy parrot.

The human play gym. Interactive companion parrots are easily enticed to play with interesting objects attached to humans and their clothing. Whether it's simply buttons or true bird toys attached to an old sweatshirt, bracelet, or eyeglasses, if

Self-rewarding Behavior

A self-rewarding behavior is anything done solely for the joy of doing it.

birds. Weaving paper, leather, or bias-cut cloth in and out of the cage bars near the bird's favorite perch can draw a bird into chewing. Bundles of twigs might be attached to the sides of the cage. Branches where the bark is already starting to peel can replace plain perches.

Games Birds Like to Play with People

In addition to toy play, parrots crave interaction with their companions. Even if a bird is frightened, cautious, or outright hostile, passive interactions can progress to increasingly interactive play.

Some parrots communicate by imitating human speech. They also learn to understand limited verbal communication from humans. The most dependable channel of communication with a parrot, however, is body language—nonverbal cues one individual gives another.

An astute owner learns to read a bird's mood by the position of the feathers. Depending upon the way they are held, ruffled head feathers may be an invitation to pet, a warning of aggression, or a sign of illness.

The companion parrot also learns to read human body language. A well-adjusted pet may be drawn to almost any personality type, but a wary new bird will more easily trust steady, placid people who don't move their heads or hands when they talk. Active children or animated

A tired, annoyed, or otherwise unfriendly parrot might demonstrate that it doesn't wish interactions by turning its back to people. (African grey parrot)

conversationalists who punctuate words with gestures can confuse and frighten shy birds.

The following games include both verbal and nonverbal passive interactions. Different parrots will favor different games. Individual pets will learn to play the games in different sequences, but all types of parrots in all stages of tameness enjoy playful, passive interaction. Humans, however, must identify and learn the games birds like to play.

Stage 1, Games for Shy Birds

I couldn't possibly look at you: Eye contact is threatening to a shy parrot, so one must mimic the bird's behavior. Look away if you catch the bird looking at you. Turn your head, cast your eyes down, or otherwise hide your eyes (*not* with hands) until the bird is comfortable looking at you and letting you look back.

I can be shorter than you: With a puppy, you play fighting/domination games like "I am bigger and tougher than you!" One may also play roughhouse games with some domestic hand-fed parrots, but most new birds (particularly wild-caught ones) prefer to play more passive games. Because a creature on a level lower than the bird is less threatening, situate yourself so your eyes are always lower than the bird's eyes.

I can be a statue: A variation of "I can be shorter." If the parrot freezes when looked at, try holding still longer than the bird. (Many cockatoos love this game!)

I am more frightened than you: You come around the corner quickly; the bird is startled, screams, and flops off the perch. Counter this reaction with body language that indicates you are more terrified than the bird (but don't scream). Make yourself very short, hide, or calm yourself by slowly rocking back and forth and by making cooing sounds. This demonstrates your own caution, which can help to gain the trust of the nervous bird.

I don't have hands: Since you are trying to impress this feathered, fingerless creature with your similarities, prevent the bird from seeing your hands. Approach a parrot in the most nonthreatening manner with your "wings" folded (hands in pockets or behind back).

Stage 2, Games for Birds that Are Somewhat Steady

Blink back: An animal experiencing fear will not blink while maintaining eye contact with an assumed aggressor. Initiate communication by making eye contact then blinking your eyes. An interested, interactive parrot will close its eyes or "blink back" with a new friend if it, too, is growing trustful. If the bird is very fearful, it will not blink while you are maintaining eye contact.

Peep-eye (peek-a-boo): A curious parrot growing accustomed to new surroundings will wonder where people go when out of sight. It might stretch to see around corners or climb around for a better view. A human friend might also peer around corners and reading materials for a look at the parrot's private activities. Try combining this game with "blink" and "I can be shorter . . . ."

I can sleep in front of you: A bird looking down on a sleeping human is not afraid. Sometimes while sneaking a peek from a reclining position, you may first observe a new bird preening, tail wagging, "shaking out" or exhibiting other happiness behaviors.

I like to touch and be touched: If you ultimately wish to caress your parrot, demonstrate the joy you feel when touching a loved one or another pet. Showing affection to others will also help your bird feel comfortable in their presence. Be cautious, because in the future this game might stimulate jealousy and overt or displaced aggression. Be sensitive to the responses you are observing.

Tap, tap, tap: Many parrots will tap a foot or beak, apparently to intimidate, or simply for attention. A respectful but unfrightened human might tap back the same rhythm with a pencil, fork, or finger. This game is the audio version of "Blink" and may be initiated by a curious, more confident bird.

Stage 3, Games for More Confident Parrots

Let's get rowdy together: Many birds will vocalize loudly along with a favorite song, an appliance, or a broadcast sports event. Bird buddies are usually eager to vocalize with each other and with noises in their environment, whether it's a living room or a jungle. Create a social bond by joining your bird in a good scream (on occasion).

I'm calling yooouuuoouu!: A curious parrot will want to know where you are, even if it cannot see you. The bird will call out, and if you answer, it will call back. This is a favorite parrot-initiated game and an excellent way to teach a bird to speak for attention. It's also a great way to teach a parrot to scream, so watch that volume.

Rituals: All birds in a flock seek food, eat, shower, groom, scream, and perform other necessary physical functions in unison. Your parrot will demonstrate its connection with you by eating when you eat, bathing when it hears running water, grooming, laughing, and screaming at the dog when you do these things. Encourage your bird to develop nonviolent, nonsexual rituals.

Stage 4, Games for Well-Socialized Companion Birds

Anything you can do, I can do, too: Once a bird feels comfortable, it will stretch, shake out, or wiggle its tongue with no reservations. A bird delights in humans who mimic these behaviors. Like a kitten, a healthy parrot will greet human friends with a long, slow stretch. Owners who observe a bird stretching a greeting by extending a wing and a leg might "parrot" the parrot's behavior. This would demonstrate a similar feeling of well-being and happiness in the company of a friend.

I can give you food, and you will eat it: Many birds will take food from a hand, then drop or throw it. Try mimicking the bird's behavior. Drop or throw the food once or twice, wait a few minutes, then offer the food again. A happy, well-adjusted bird will accept food and eat it. If the bird will not take food from your hand *and eat it*, go back to Stage 1 or 2.

I'll drop it, and you pick it up: Quite possibly, this is the game most frequently initiated by parrots with humans. Almost every parrot owner can relate a story or two about this most frustrating game. Some people will play it, and some people are just too proud. I believe any human who will spend a few moments picking up a repeatedly dropped trinket for a bird is well on the way to being a trusted, treasured friend for life.

I will wear toys for you: All tame birds know that eyeglasses, jewelry, buttons, and shoelaces are worn solely for *their* entertainment. Carry hold-and-chew toys to substitute for unapproved chewables when socializing with your bird. For safety's sake, select pierced earrings with backs that pop off easily, and don't expect to have easy-to-thread shoelaces. Those little plastic tips resemble new feather sheaths and will be promptly removed if accessible.

Tug-o-war: It's not okay to let the bird win *all the time*, particularly if it is an aggressive bird; but be sure to let a shy bird win often.

Rescue me!: Also a favorite parrot-initiated game with several frightening variations. *Help, my toe is caught!* is a version well loved and frequently played by Amazons. It was certainly the favorite game of Portia, my yellow nape, during his bachelor days. (Yes—this Portia proved to be a male!) He would flap, scream, and hang upside down by a single toe. When his concerned owner rushed to help, she found a delighted bird (not stuck) gleefully displaying for attention. This game is exciting, though a little hard on the heart. A loving owner must check the bird in case it really is in trouble!

Chase me!: This is a slightly controversial game because it isn't passive, and one must be sure that *the bird* wants to play. (Never chase a frightened parrot if you have a choice.) The concept of this game is that there is running and chasing, *but no catching*.

Chase Me! is a favorite game of Goffin's cockatoos and is sometimes mistaken for fearful or untame behavior. I am often called to tame a "bronco" Goffin's whose owners are convinced that the bird doesn't like them. "She comes to me, but when I try to touch her, she takes off like a shot," confused humans say.

Usually, I find a doting bird that runs from even the most mundane contacts—not in fear, but for fun. Some Goffin's will literally run circles around the person they want to chase them. If you want to handle these little beauties, entice them with passive body language, wait and reward them—with petting, not food—for coming to you.

A parrot's games vary with the passing of time from shy baby games to more sophisticated challenges and flirtations. These interactions will remain a delightful part of your lives together. Playful passive interactions are a great way to relate to a tame parrot that needs attention when everyone is too busy to handle it.

Passive noncontact games are absolutely the best way to interact with a bird that doesn't like being touched. Simply because a parrot won't tolerate hands doesn't mean it isn't a playful pet. Certainly, the more creativity and imagination you devote to a pet's games, the more enjoyable will be your time together.

How to Pet a Parrot

When the hand is presented, a tame parrot will step up on it. A "teddy bear" bird will fluff its neck feathers and tuck its head under or against the hand for petting. What a joy it is when your bird nuzzles its head under your finger for the first time!

When introducing a parrot to the joys of petting, the bird's enjoyment of the process is the most important factor, so obvious domination techniques usually don't work well; in fact, they might do more harm than good. Perserverance is involved, gentle and subtle—more like a dance or seduction. The bird is introduced to a gradually increasing level of pleasure that overcomes its natural aversion to physical contact with humans.

Practice: Teaching a reluctant bird to enjoy touching requires a practiced, accomplished bird petter versed in avian pleasure techniques. These are acquired skills that can be learned by petting birds that already enjoy human touch. Tame Moluccan and umbrella cockatoos are commonly "teddy bear" birds and willing participants in petting practice.

Usually, most parrots do not naturally enjoy petting in the directions feathers grow. Not only does it offer little sensation, but the feeling it affords replicates their "wary" expression (the holding of feathers smoothly against the body).

Most hookbills prefer petting gently across or against the direction of feather growth. To understand how this feels, run your hand along the surface of your hair in the direction of growth. Then insert fingers under your hair and gently caress both across the direction of growth and against the direction of growth. Which is more pleasing?

It is not important to touch the skin. Since feather shafts are rigid, it is necessary only to move feathers in the appropriate direction to induce pleasure; this can be done with the breath. Even if a bird likes a little skin contact, move from place to place to avoid irritation.

Blood feathers or pin feathers (the ones that still have a blood supply) must be petted gently with or across the feathers. This means that a bird that normally enjoys petting against the feathers may prefer with-the-feather petting during molting. This phenomenon is not to be underestimated. Some birds really like to be petted with the feathers, although many merely tolerate it because it's the only way they get petted at all. The sensitivity of the petter to evaluate the bird's response is most important here. Mary Kaye Buchtel reports that *Eclectus* parrots, in particular, prefer with-the-feather petting.

Most birds react negatively to touching of wing and tail feathers. Also avoid the breast to avoid confusion with the *step-up* prompt. Almost any other place on the body might be considered an erogenous zone by a typical parrot. Pay special attention to ears, nostrils, eye rings, beak, under the beak, wing pit, the bony ridges along top underside of wings, under the tail, on top of the tail (oil gland),

Like this umbrella cockatoo, many parrots commonly enjoy being petted under the feathers of the head.

or about midway and roll or slide fingers toward the tip. This is particularly effective in the presence of blood feathers, as a solitary pet bird usually has no bird buddy to "unwrap" incoming new feathers. The casing on a mature blood feather should be broken off no closer than ⅓ inch (.8 cm) from the blood supply. This approximates a bird behavior called alopreening.

Observe: A parrot experiencing pleasure will fluff up the feathers on the area being caressed. It may close its eyes or make appreciative noises. Although the bird will be very still, it may alter its position to accommodate petting in desired areas. When successful hand contact is discontinued, there will be happiness behaviors—puffing feathers, shaking out body or wings, and tail wagging. A completely mesmerized bird will remain motionless when petting is discontinued.

A parrot inviting petting may strike a glazed, come-hither look, puff up its neck feathers, and lower the head. An untame parrot may exhibit postures inviting contact, then react badly when you try to touch it.

Because many parrots fear or dislike gloves (because of handling as they are shipped or in pet stores) and towels (because of physical exams or grooming), begin petting training by containing a reluctant parrot in a down vest or jacket. Almost any garment will do, although it may wind up with a hole or two.

Cradle the bird gently within the garment and pet it with hands hidden

and the neck. Many cockatoos enjoy being gently stroked on the bald spot under their crest. Most birds who enjoy petting like a little squeeze from a hand cupped under the wings and over the back. Be careful with this one, though, because many birds find this sexually stimulating and may develop aggressive tendencies.

The jaw is a particular favorite of most parrots. Wiggle a finger along the lower edge of the jawbone; approaching the lower mandible, the bird may turn its head upside down to accommodate the finger. Larger parrots may appreciate a little probing into the cavity under the lower beak where the tongue rests when the beak is closed. Some cooperative birds will yawn when petted in a circular motion at the intersection of upper and lower jawbones.

Spend time gently pulling the feathers. Grasp them near the base

from sight. It is probably unnecessary to actually restrain the bird in the garment, as most soon realize they really enjoy petting. Never restrict the in-and-out movement of the bird's chest.

Speak softly and constantly, slipping a bare hand up to pet under or over the base of the tail. Try to pet the bird's cheek, nostrils, or jaw without it seeing fingers.

Observation and sensitivity are the keys to success in this project. Because this technique works for some birds and not others, be sensitive to the bird's behavior and prepare to modify the approach if the bird's response is negative.

Don't push too hard, but don't back off too soon and reinforce resistance on the part of the bird. Watch for the absence or presence of happiness behaviors such as preening or tail wagging when hand contact is removed.

Again, it is not necessary to actually pet a bird on the skin, but merely to move the feathers, which may be done with a warm, gentle breath directed to the neck.

A bird that will allow foot stroking may then permit petting up the thighs, under or over the tail, along the back to the neck but without touching the wings. I believe many "touch freak" birds first learn to hold their wings up for wing-pit petting because their first instinct is to raise them to avoid having their wings touched during petting.

Pet, then *back off and observe*. If the bird expresses a happiness

The Head Squeeze

Many birds enjoy what essentially amounts to a cranial massage. This "head squeeze" can be accomplished like this: while engaging in neck and heat petting, slide the thumb over one ear, index and middle finger back over the head, knuckle of ring finger over the other ear and gently squeeze. Feel the shape of the skull and jaw. Some birds will become totally mesmerized by this special massage technique.

response (shake out and/or tail wag) within two minutes, continue. If the bird looks uncomfortable and/or tries to get away, then try a different approach or go more slowly. This learn-to-be-petted process must not be interpreted by the bird as domination, but rather enticement.

Some birds respond to being petted on the oil gland on top of the tail at the base of the spine. Insert fingers under and into the feathers for maximum pleasure and also to hide them from the bird's sight. From the area of the oil gland, proceed under wings or up the backbone to the neck and head.

On a training stand: Some hand-shy birds tolerate petting with a pencil or other small inanimate object. A bird on a chest-level training stand may be distracted with one hand and touched with the other. If the bird looks at one hand, approach with the other. Touch the bird briefly in a place where petting is usually

Like this blue-crowned mealy Amazon, *a parrot may offer the jaw to be scratched under the feathers. As with head or neck petting, this might feel similar to alopreening by another bird.*

displaying shy and sensitive body language while becoming progressively more bold.

Watch for signs of regression—less passive interaction, excessive biting, or refusing favorite treats on a regular basis. Back off if the bird is not showing improved tolerance and/or enjoyment of petting. Give more rewards, go more slowly, and start over. Don't pressure the bird or repeatedly force it to do something it doesn't want to do.

Modeling: A hand-shy bird might be induced to allow petting if it observes another bird enjoying petting. If no other bird is available, try petting another person. Have a human "second student" compete for attention when you are trying to pet the bird; then notice the second student, spend time petting and softly speaking to the second student, and watch the bird's reaction.

Don't underestimate the value of soft lights and sweet music. No matter how wild the parrot, woo gently, and the cuddles will come.

enjoyed by other similar types of birds, then gradually increase contact time.

Reward: Accompany each handling session with generous rewards of loving words, showers, or treats. Some trainers withhold favorite food items—grapes, sunflower seeds, peanuts, or peppers—from the bird's normal diet except from the hand.

Reaction: A bird may temporarily discontinue taking favorite foods. Demonstrative birds may snatch the treat, then drop or throw it. Try mimicking their behavior, that is, drop or throw the treat, wait a few minutes, then offer the treat again. This phase should pass within a few days or something is wrong.

Again, this process is more like a courtship, with the human teacher

The Formation of Habits

When we do something for the first time, assemble a bicycle or operate a computer program, it is often terribly difficult and time consuming. Each time we go through the motions of a task, that activity becomes both easier and faster, until after a time, the patterned activity is not only easier to

Petting on the underside of the wing is less sexually stimulating and, therefore, more beneficial than petting on the back under the wing. (umbrella cockatoo)

do, but it actually becomes difficult to do something different. This can be defined as habitual behavior. If a parrot or a human is habitually cantankerous and uncooperative, we must expect that individual to repeat the same or similar behaviors. Any time a bird bites a human, it is easier for that bird to bite that human next time.

If a parrot or a human is habitually cooperative, we can expect cooperative behavior throughout all areas of the bird's behavior. Each time a bird peacefully interacts with humans, it is easier for the bird to interact peacefully the next time. Maintaining peaceful behavior in a parrot is dependent upon the regular practice and performance of redundant, interactive rituals or routines that both the bird and the humans enjoy.

Any repeated enjoyable interaction between human and bird can establish cooperation in their relationship and be a part of the bird's routine way of relating. The most practical and easily accessible exercises for accomplishing this are peek-a-boos, step-ups, and the towel game. Peek-a-boos are universal, played by juvenile animals of all kinds. You don't have to be in the same room. Just peek around a corner and say something cute and appropriate like, "Peek-a-boo!" or "Peek-a-bird!"

Early reinforcement of the bird's step-up response is the groundwork for peaceful handling. The bird should enjoy stepping on and off of a hand as well as onto and off of a hand-held perch. If the bird doesn't step up easily at the cage, then practice in unfamiliar territory. Be sure to offer the perch where the legs join the belly so that it is easily reached with the feet, rather than the beak. Be sure to maintain eye contact rather than looking at the approaching hand. If the bird is maintaining eye contact and you look at your hand, the bird will look at your hand. If the bird looks at the approaching hand, it might either bite or flee rather than step up.

All cooperation patterning must be enjoyable to the bird. Practice of this interaction establishes the teacher as a flock member who should be looked to as a model for behavior. The step-up response must be so well entrenched that the bird will automatically perform the behavior, even if it is focused on biting, stealing a ring, sitting in a treetop, or being rescued from a fire. The bird should be so well practiced that when you say "Step-up," no matter what is happening, it will immediately discontinue whatever it is doing and lift that foot!

Step-ups

In the relatively new field of companion parrot behavior management, step-up exercises were the first behavioral tool to be described as a patterning tool. From its first days in the home, the baby parrot should enjoy practicing step-ups a little bit every day.

Although we may be able to begin step-up practice with a cooperative baby bird in familiar territory, unless a bird is cooperative enough and well patterned enough to step up

from an unfamiliar perch in unfamiliar territory, it may refuse to step up from the cage or other familiar perch.

A formal routine need be no more than one or two minutes' duration and may initially have to take place outside the bird's established territory in the home. A laundry room or hallway is usually perfect, as the bird will probably never spend much time in these types of areas, and therefore should not develop territorial behavior in them. A cooperative bird can be successfully patterned to this exercise anywhere. The routine is most effective when it includes

1. practice stepping the bird from the hand to and from an unfamiliar perch,

2. practice stepping the bird from a hand to another hand,

3. practice stepping the bird from a hand-held perch to and from an unfamiliar perch,

4. practice stepping the bird from a hand-held perch to a hand-held perch, and

5. practice stepping the bird from a familiar perch to and from both hands and to and from hand-held perches.

Once the cooperative bird enjoys all aspects of the above-described routine, it is not necessary to do the whole thing every day. Just vary the use of hands and hand-held perches and the location of the spontaneous practice routines so that the bird happily maintains good interactions with both hands and perches.

Be sure to offer food, affection, or praise after each completed step-up.

Always discontinue step-up practice after a successful completion of the command. This is crucial to good patterning. If the command is not successful or if the bird is not enjoying the process, we must alter technique, approach, or prompting mannerisms rather than continue with unsuccessful methods. We must be careful not to reinforce unsuccessful patterns.

There is no substitute for warm, genuine human enthusiasm as a reward for the bird's success in stepping up. Especially with shy or cautious birds, the most important part of this exercise is probably the bird's enjoyment of the process. If the bird is not eagerly, or at least willingly, cooperating with step-ups and step-up practice, something is going wrong; and the owner should look for professional help immediately.

The Towel Game

This might be called "peeking out" patterning. It is an easy way to access a sense of safety for both birds and humans (towel-covered hands are more difficult to bite). The towel game really is not like restraining a bird in a towel for physical examination, it is more like playing peek-a-boo under the covers, only you use a towel instead of a blanket (the bigger the towel the better, so that at first one or more humans can get under there too). Just try to make the bird feel happy and secure and let it peek out (cavity breeders spend a lot of time peeking out of small

Cockatoos take to towel training like ducks take to water. (umbrella cockatoo)

spaces) and sometimes hide the bird's head or eyes and then expose them and say, "peek-a-bird."

Begin by modeling the towel game with anyone and everyone except the bird in the towel. Sit low, across the room from the bird and hide your face with the towel, then lower the towel, peek around it, and blink, giggle, or say "peek-a-bird."

Also, try being the "mysterious creature" in the towel. At a time when the bird is in a great mood, preferably after a well-enjoyed bath, and ready to mellow out, wear a fluffy clean terry cloth bath robe (no stripes), and wear a towel colored like the bird over your head, partially obscuring your face like very long hair. Let the edges of the towel stick out several inches from your face so that your face is mostly obscured. Let the ends of the towel hang down with two corners touching in the middle front and the other two corners behind your shoulders so that your face is inside and there is sort of a cave under your chin. Try whistling, singing, dancing, and holding out the

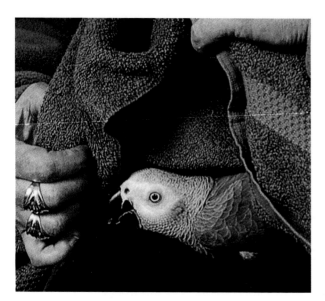

front corners of the towel, one in each hand, sort of like a bird holding out it is wings to catch rainfall. Play lots of eye games and peek-a-boos, and act like a parrot enjoying a shower. (You are trying to convince this prey species that you are also a prey species, not an evil predator.)

You will notice that if you just let the ends of the towel hang down like long hair and then bend your head forward, there is a large cave under your face. With the bird on a comfortable low perch, maybe a chair back, try to lean over the bird so that the ends of the towel come forward opening the "cave" that you are in so the bird can be in there too. Keep your hands covered by the towel so that the bird never sees hands.

Flirt with the bird with eyes and body when you are inside the towel, play peek-a-boos, and sometimes let another person or bird or pet in there

without the bird to play with you. You might take one of the bird's favorite holding toys inside the towel and make lots of fun noises while playing with it. Sometimes you and another person could play with the bird's favorite toy inside the towel. If the bird is very food motivated, you could let it see you eating a favorite food inside the towel.

Soon, you will be able to put the bird on its regular step-up practice perch, maybe a chair back, in unfamiliar territory, and, approaching with the towel draped over both hands from below, gently surround the bird with the towel. At first, you do not even have to pick the bird up, but the approach from below is extremely important. If the bird is approached from above, the towel can stimulate a feeling of being attacked by a predator. Later, you can step the bird up on to a towel-covered hand or scoop up the bird enfolded in the towel and snuggle it like an infant.

Eventually, you will be able to cover only the bird's head with the towel, and the bird will think it is inside the towel. Then you can pet any known-to-be-enjoyable place that the bird cannot see. (The neck is a good place to start, of course.)

Another way to start is with the towel laid over your lap with the long ends hanging down on each side. Put the bird on your lap and put one hand under each end of the towel. Lift the ends of the towel up to the sides of your face, making a sort of canyon or cavern with the bird and your face inside. At first you do not have to put your hands together; but you can eventually, and you can drape each end of the towel over the bird and then start looking for the bird and playing "peek-a-bird."

Actually, there is no "wrong" way to play peek-a-bird if the bird is interacting and enjoying the process! It is just peeking around corners with "flexible corners."

It's usually easier to teach a baby bird to enjoy the towel game than to teach an older bird. However, older birds often naturally "enjoy" spending time in restricting enclosures, such as a nest box. It is not unusual for even a retired breeding bird to be easily conditioned to absolutely adore the towel game.

Distractions

Part of the charm of companion parrots is their tendency to interact differently with different people. That is, a companion parrot might be nice as pie to some people in the home and might routinely nip or bite others who try to handle it with different techniques. Ideally, all humans interacting with the bird should be trained in use of the same techniques, as companion parrots will respond to the same stimuli with the same behavior and to different stimuli with different behaviors.

The wobble correction is a distraction device (not a punishment!) commonly used when the nipping or biting bird is sitting on a hand or on a hand-held perch. It is best employed just before the bird nips or bites; it may also be used just as the nip occurs. The hand or perch that the bird is sitting on (not the one being nipped) is gently and quickly wobbled so that the bird must momentarily pay attention in order to regain balance. This is usually best accomplished by quickly tipping the outside end of the hand or hand-held perch first down and then back up. The bird will have to discontinue whatever it was doing to retain grip and balance. Be sure to maintain eye contact and remind the bird either to *"Be a good bird"* or to *"Be careful."*

A behavior that is not reinforced does not become a permanent fixture. As the bird tests the use of the beak on flesh, it might become necessary to respond a little more directly to test nips occurring during step-up practice. First, be sure that the hand is being offered properly, coming from below and just over the feet near the place where the leg joins the belly rather than approaching from the front toward the breast or beak. Then, if the bird nips the hand being offered, quickly dip the fingers of the hand the bird is sitting on (not the hand being offered and nipped) then return the hand to its former position. This must be accomplished carefully so that the bird does not fall or become fearful during the process.

The bird will have to discontinue a nip in order to regain balance. It will soon understand that nips during step-ups cause "earthquakes." This distraction must be delivered quickly,

Distraction Devices

A bird might decide to bite even a well-placed hand prompt for step-ups. The most common time for a nip or bite of a hand offered for a step-up is when the bird is being removed from a familiar perch, the inside or top of the cage, or when it is being returned to the cage. This behavior can usually be defeated with a hand-held perch, improved technique, or more frequent step-up practice in unfamiliar territory.

Sometimes a distraction device is necessary to keep the bird from looking at the hand approaching for the step-up. Maintain eye contact and offer the hand to be stepped on, approaching from below, as usual. Just as the prompt hand begins its approach to the bird, present an unfamiliar object just out of reach of the bird's beak (with one hand) and give the "step up" command (with the other hand) followed by, *"Be a good bird."*

That is, if a bird is threatening to bite when stepping up, I can pick up a small object (a spoon or telephone or piece of junk mail) and hold it about an inch below and in front of the bird's beak, give the step-up command, and suggest good behavior. Usually the surprised bird, responding to the familiar behavioral pattern, and knowing what "good bird" means, also responds by being what it is expected to be (a good bird).

Eye contact is important here. A bird will maintain eye contact rather than bite. If the bird's eye is distracted by the introduced object, it will seek to regain eye contact immediately rather than take the time to bite after being distracted. Even if the bird bites, that unfamiliar object, rather than the hand being offered, will probably be bitten. A clean new wooden spoon or handheld toy works well for this. Take care to ensure that the distraction device is not frightening to a shy parrot. The distraction object must be neither too large (which might frighten the bird), too small (which might be ineffective), nor toxic (a lead or painted object) if the bird chooses to receive the object and chew on it.

gently, and sensitively so that the bird is not overly affected either physically or emotionally.

"Good Hand/Bad Hand"

We might choose to pick up an otherwise-well-adapted bird either with hand-held perches or not handle it at all during nippy stages. Don't discontinue all interaction, just discontinue interactions that might facilitate biting; that might mean discontinuing anything that involves touching the bird. Go back to passive games (page 35). Practice stimulating and reinforcing wanted behavior.

Avoid interaction when a parrot signals intent to bite by pinpointing the eye, leaning toward you with feathers smooth, beak open and feet wide, firmly gripping the perch. (male eclectus protected by female)

Thoughtful, consistent technique by everyone interacting with the bird is necessary to maintain tameness here, for if the bird has no chance to bite, biting can't be reinforced.

If a parrot has not been socialized by the teen years, attempts to socialize may be dominated by the bird's instincts to reproduce and by habitual self-rewarding behaviors that have developed. During the teen years a parrot might develop both predictable and unpredictable biting behavior, especially in perceived territory. There is usually plenty of warning: hyper-vigilance, eye movement, wing or tail display, charging with beak open, or other body language showing impending aggression from that individual.

The best way to deal with biting in a sexually mature companion parrot is to avoid it. Do anything necessary to stimulate different behavior. Never

allow the bird to chase or harass people or animals. Just clap your hands for attention, say, *"Be a good bird,"* then return the bird to the cage in the calmest possible way. Distract from a threatened bite during the step-up prompt with a toy, towel, magazine, or other inanimate object.

Even solitary parrots can develop sexual behaviors. Although many companion parrots express more sexual-display or courtship behaviors—including chewing, eating, and feeding—other birds will more overtly seek sexual gratification. Expect to see masturbation in many healthy male birds and some female birds. A companion parrot might solicit copulation from a favorite human or engage in masturbation, masturbation display, or anxiety behaviors that sometimes include masturbation or copulation postures. Each bird's masturbation process is accompanied by

Sandee Molenda could tell the man on the other end of the phone line was dismayed to hear her obviously female voice.

"Is Robert there?" He paused, cleared his throat. "I have an unusual parrotlet question."

"I can help you." Sandee smiled.

Following another pause and a deep sigh, he began. "I have a two-year old male Pacific and he's...um, he is, ah, ...um..., seems to be, umm..., rubbing... um, ..."

She gently interrupted. "Well, sir, he *is* doing what you think he's doing, but not to worry, he won't go blind."

that species' characteristic sounds, which an astute owner learns to recognize. This is similar to my own hen cockatiel Pearl's behavior, who neither talks nor whistles except as she masturbates, in the corner of her cage (see page 31).

These behaviors should not be reinforced, as they can be accompanied by aggression or feather picking. A habitually masturbating parrot may later choose those behaviors over mating even if a mate is offered. Just ignore these behaviors. If the behaviors don't get attention and aren't reinforced, they're less likely to reappear. However, since self-gratification is the very definition of self-rewarding behavior, sexual behaviors may continue regardless of whether or not they have been reinforced.

Potty Training

Cookie, an umbrella cockatoo, was always naturally potty trained. Rescued from murderous parents at three days old, he seemed to have an intuitive understanding that he shouldn't relieve himself on people. The now-adult Cookie has never dirtied human clothing with his droppings.

Cookie is unusually perceptive; but potty-trained parrots are becoming less and less uncommon. While cockatoos and macaws are believed to be the easiest, even cockatiels are trainable. As our understanding of parrot behavior increases, so does our ability to modify that behavior. Indeed, many bird people believe that potty training a parrot may be easier than accomplishing the same feat in a male puppy (although owner motivation is not the same).

In the past, potty training birds was in widespread disfavor among caring aviculturists, for although it is easy to train a parrot to defecate on verbal command, this method is dangerous. Occasionally, a bird may be so eager to please that it will incur life-threatening kidney damage waiting for that verbal command. This becomes an issue if the owner is ill or injured or must go out of town. A forgotten instruction to command the bird to defecate has proved fatal on at least one documented occasion.

Potty training a companion parrot involves reaching an understanding on the appropriate place to leave that dropping. One may safely train a bird to an approved location (cage or play area) or a visual stimulus—paper. You must then be sure that the bird has either continuous access to the approved location or paper or that the bird is handled in a manner to accommodate the elimination schedule.

It works like this: each time you want to pick up the bird, place it on its perch or over paper until it eliminates. Some birds do this automatically when first handled. Play with the bird or just keep it with you for about 20 to 30 minutes. Before the bird eliminates again, place it on or over the paper until it goes. Then reward the bird with food or affection.

It helps to know the approximate length of time between droppings. Observation and sensitivity are the keys to this process. You will soon notice changes in the bird's behavior shortly before elimination: the tail will wiggle, the bird will become fidgety. When it is time to defecate, be sure the bird can get to the paper.

It is difficult to remember *not* to say the same thing every time you are waiting for the bird to eliminate. If you repeatedly say something like, "Any time now, dummy," your pet will associate those words with the elimination response, and you will be incorrectly and dangerously training to a verbal command.

Potty training a small parrot like a cockatiel is just as easy as potty training a large one like this Amazon.

Also remember, a parrot can't tell one piece of paper from another, so don't leave important documents lying around. No paper will be safe; but clothes, furniture, and carpeting will be spared a little of the never-ending cleaning.

Chapter Four
Ongoing Behavior Management

A companion parrot has the opportunity to study individual roles, group dynamics, physical components, and housekeeping processes much more thoroughly than any other single family member. The bird's needs and sense of participation can give rise to some startling intended and unintended consequences in human living spaces. Even the most watchful humans may have difficulty identifying factors contributing to the bird's ongoing behavioral development.

A well-adapted parrot in a well-equipped cage is never bored. (African grey)

A Bird Needs a Cage

Many common behavior problems in companion parrots may be traced to lack of a suitable cage. The problems are not usually directly caused by lack of a cage. They may be the result of stress compounded by lack of a suitable cage, inappropriate bonding to a person or place due to lack of a cage, lack of exercise, interrupted sleep periods, inappropriate photo periods, harassment by a cage mate, or any one of several other physical and social processes.

Feather chewing, screaming, apathy, aggression, displaced aggression, and sudden nipping are often (but not exclusively) associated with lack of a cage or ill-suited caging. Unacceptable behaviors may develop because of poor adjustment to the color, shape, location, or height of a cage. Failure to provide a cage during the developmental period can lead to many difficult-to-correct problem behaviors.

One of the most common causes of cage-related behavior problems in companion parrots is failure to provide a cage. Surely, a bird needs an open perch or play gym, but a bird also needs a cage.

A room of one's own: Whether a bird is so gregarious it's always into everything or so shy it seeks privacy, a roomy cage out of traffic is needed for good long-term emotional health. A shy bird requires security; a social bird must learn to play alone, thereby preventing the development of dominance behaviors through demands for attention. A bird doing poorly in a shared cage may need to be isolated for protection from abuse by other birds.

A personal gymnasium: A healthy bird is an active bird. Most pet parrots—for reasons of safety and habit—express their energy through climbing, swinging, and flapping.

A bird on a 2-foot long (60-cm) open perch has only 2 *lateral* feet (60 cm) in which to walk back and forth. Adding a 4-foot (1.2-m) rope triples the space to 6 feet (2 m) of climbing and flapping space. A cage only 2 feet square has 4 square feet (.37 m²) on every side and the top— 20 *square feet* (1.8 m²) inside and 20 *square feet* (1.8 m²) outside—a total of *40 square feet (3.7 m³) of climbing space!* There is 20 times more climbing surface on a 2 by 2 by 2-foot (60 × 60 × 60-cm) cage than on a 2-foot (60-cm) open perch. Of course, you cannot put a full-sized macaw in a 2 by 2 by 2-foot cage and you can put a macaw on a 2-foot perch. It is a less than ideal situation that should not be considered permanent housing.

Intermittent reinforcement of existing behavior ensures that it will be repeated. (yellow-naped Amazon)

A corner to hang out on: Parrots with nonaggressive territorial tendencies may be housed with the cage door open almost all the time. However, at first remove the bird from the cage on your hand in order to maintain social dominance. A well-adjusted bird will spend a good deal of time sitting on the cage on the corner closest to people when there might be a little attention to be had; but it will eat, drink, sleep, and entertain itself inside and outside the cage.

Size: If the cage is the only place the bird has to spend the majority of its time, that cage should be very large indeed, with width and depth and height all being at least 1½ times the bird's extended wingspan. If the cage is smaller than that, the bird

A companion parrot that spends time on many different "foraging areas" around the home is less likely to aggressively defend territory. (blue and gold macaw)

should be provided with a foraging or commuting lifestyle.

Configuration: The shape of the cage should include corners. Some birds will be noisy, self-mutilating, phobic, or otherwise ill-at-ease in a round

Many parrots need especially designed food and water dishes that cannot be moved or dumped by the bird.

or cylindrical cage. Also, avoid a cage with a solid top. Choose one with a wire top or one composed of bars.

Territory: I do not recommend the cage as the only approved location for a companion parrot to spend time. During most of the year, territorialism, not sexual fugues, appears to be the primary motivation for aggression in medium and larger hookbills. In captivity there appears to be a direct relationship between the amount of space a parrot commands and the intensity with which that territory is defended—the smaller the space, the greater the fervor with which that territory is defended.

Commuting: Unless the cage is the only approved play area, it should be situated well away from human activity areas so that the bird's sleep periods are not interrupted by human activities. A roosting cage might not have much space for silliness, flapping, and climbing. Daily outings to a play area must be provided. This is an excellent opportunity to build a "dependency relationship" with the bird wherein it relies on its less favorite human companions to provide transportation daily from the "roost" or sleeping cage to the "foraging area" or playpen.

I believe birds are less likely to become aggressively territorial when they are kept as "commuters" who move frequently from a private roost to a mobile "foraging" area that goes wherever the "flock" goes. A big unpainted basket with the handle wrapped in jute, well-fitted with dishes and toys, and weighted with newspapers is an easy-to-live-with portable foraging area.

Acquisition of a suitable cage and sensitively introducing the bird to the new cage will frequently correct related behavior problems of less than one year's duration. Even a roosting cage that houses the bird at night and infrequently during a part of the day should be at least 1½ times wider than the bird's extended wing span in at least one direction. It should have a tray at least 2 inches (5 cm) deep. Food and water dishes should be accessible to servicing from outside the cage; and if the bird likes to tear up stuff in the bottom of the cage, there should be a grill at least 1 or 2 inches (2.5–5 cm) above the tray.

Introducing a new cage: Although many birds exhibit immediate and delighted response to a new cage, some birds must be enticed to accept a new cage. In the face of reluctance, place the cage in the bird's favorite place and set the old cage on the floor lower than the new cage with a branch or ladder between them. After a day or so, remove food and water dishes, then a day or two later remove the perches from the old cage. Place food and water dishes on top of the new cage, then gradually move them inside the cage. An older bird that has been in the same cage for many years—even if it is a small inadequate cage—may have strong emotional ties that must be broken gradually over a period of time. The object of the new cage is to reduce stress, not cause it, so give the bird at least a couple of days before removing that old cage.

A Bird's Gotta Chew What a Bird's Gotta Chew

Particularly in the time of year perceived by companion birds to be "springtime," our feathered friends use their beaks to reduce everything they can reach to toothpicks (in the case of small parrots, confetti). Along with annual screaming and hormonal rites, parrots are eagerly expressing their sexuality by demonstrating their cavity-building (demolition) skills.

I am often asked to correct chewing behaviors. These are some of my favorite calls, for the remedy, though ever so tricky, is easily accessible to *most* parrot owners.

Anticipation: Just as a caring owner knows the dog needs a bone, a parrot owner knows the bird needs something to chew. A busy bird is a happy bird, and chewing is a major form of parrot entertainment. Controlling destructive chewing is accomplished by anticipating the bird's needs and providing appropriate chewables. Lovebirds, cockatiels, and budgies like the cardboard rolls from inside paper towels. Larger hookbills like clean wood scraps (*not pressure treated*) from the home workshop.

A variety of textures and densities are desirable, but wooden toys of medium hardness encourage just the right amount of chewing instinct. Very soft wood chewables too readily stimulate the bird's reproductive instincts, and very hard chewables eventually

prove boring (although one or two hardwood toys will prevent your having to replace all toys weekly).

While wood, and hard nuts including coconut, are favored, resilient (not brittle) plastic and very strong Plexiglas® are also fun for an enterprising hookbill. Chains of plastic shower curtain rings will stand up to some birds, but the more costly toys in the pet store are worth more because they are made to safely withstand those relentless beaks.

Kaku, a lesser sulfur cockatoo, can destroy a set of shower curtain rings in a day, but those heavy plastic chains from the pet store keep her busy for a week or so. It is particularly important to keep Kaku entertained, because if she's bored (like many of her kind) she chews her own feathers. It's not a pretty hobby! Destructible toys help prevent the onset of feather chewing for most birds. In the case of a bird that can destroy a toy in min-

utes, indestructible toys supplemented with destructible toys are necessary to control the boredom that sets in when the toy is "finished."

Be sure the bird is merely destroying the toy, not swallowing it. If there is any question about whether a bird is ingesting chewed-off portions of an inorganic toy, the toy should be allowed only with supervision. Design the environment to ensure that chewed up bits of wood, cardboard, or leather wind up on the floor rather than in the water bowl.

Controlled accessibility: If someone reports that their bird is chewing up the picture frame, lamp shade, chair, banister, or baskets, it's obvious that the bird is very much loved, or it wouldn't have access to the picture frame, chair, baskets, and the like. But respecting each other's space and property is an important part of a successful long-term relationship, and a relationship with a parrot has the potential to span generations.

You deserve to have your things respected by the bird just as surely as the bird has a right to its own space and things. That is not to say that the bird should be isolated. An isolated bird will develop screaming behaviors, become self-mutilating, or will emotionally withdraw into a zombielike state. The bird must be trained to stay in a "parrot-proofed" area not unlike a toddler's playpen. A bird with trimmed wing feathers that has not been allowed to roam is easily trained to stay in an open play area.

Put the bird on a stimulating play gym designed without easy accessibility to the floor. Provide plenty of toys and entertainment. If the bird leaves the play area, lock it in its cage for a short time. Be sure there is as much food, water, and stimulation on the play area as there is in the cage, lest the bird start "acting out" to get to the cage.

A "dual area" play space—perhaps two perches side by side or a hanging play gym linked to a floor perch by a knotted rope, or two hanging baskets connected with a rope—is sometimes helpful in training the bird to stay put. This works by providing the bird an acceptable choice of location.

When training the bird to stay on the playpen, be watchful. If it looks as if the bird is going to try to roam, clap your hands loudly and say "Be a *good bird!*" This reminder with familiar words should suggest appropriate behavior and stimulates the bird to terminate the undesirable behavior. This suggestion may be reinforced with your display to attract the bird's attention, such as a clap of the hands. This also reinforces cooperation and your role as leader. Hand the bird a toy or treat to take its mind off roaming. With a very few repetitions properly administered, most individual birds will figure out that they must stay in the play area unless invited elsewhere.*

---

*Among the most difficult-to-contain roamers and chewers are the small cockatoos (Goffin's, bare-eyes, lessers, rosies) and the full-sized macaws. They are often escape artists. I can't tell you how many parrots I've met named Houdini!

Distraction: It is extremely important for that beak to have something to chew on *all the time*. It is sometimes helpful to withhold some special chewable or to keep some favorites in reserve as a distraction for that special time when the obsession to explore and chew is strongest.

Actual physical punishment does not usually work with birds; it merely frightens, injures, or enrages them and does nothing to modify their behavior. Some people punish almost any "misbehavior" in a pet parrot with sensory deprivation: covering or isolation. In the case of chewing, which is, of course, *not* a misbehavior, I believe anticipation, controlled accessibility, and distraction are not only more humane, but ultimately more effective. Reward a quiet, busy parrot enjoying its own space with words, petting, food treats, or toys. A properly trained or contained bird provided with lots of options and an ever-evolving supply of varied, approved chewables will have no opportunity or need to eat Grandma's 150-year-old clock or the new entertainment center.

Exercise and the Companion Parrot

When a companion parrot is denied appropriate exercise both its health and behavior are affected. A healthy parrot has an enormous amount of energy. As in humans, if that energy is not expressed through physical activity, it must come out somehow. Ade-

The Benefits of Exercise

A bird following an exercise program may exhibit unexpected benefits. A few years ago I visited a client who complained that his 2½-year-old greenwing macaw "danced" constantly when he was in the room. Although the bird was not screaming, the incessant hyperactivity was maddening to the owner. I suggested responding to the behavior with "aerobics": placing the bird on the hand, moving the hand down with just enough speed to require the bird to flap its wings until it was slightly winded. At first, the bird was able to do aerobics for about 15 seconds at a time. Within a few weeks it was up to 40 seconds. Within a few months, the first three primary flight feathers, which had been damaged since the bird was a baby, were showing signs of regrowth. The end feathers on one wing had been pronounced permanently "lost" by two eminently qualified avian veterinarians; but apparently, improved circulation to the wings stimulated the follicles, after two years, to regrow feathers. The owner was happy to report that the bird discontinued the demanding behavior and learned to play alone.

quate physical activity can reduce or eliminate behaviors such as screaming, biting, feather chewing, failure to bathe, failure to groom, excessive demands for attention, and compulsive masturbation, not to mention obesity and related poor cardiovascular condition in tame companion bids.

Flapping is the exercise of choice for the most effective use of bird energy. Exercise might or might not include the human partner. A well-adjusted avian companion provided with enough space and equipment will usually, but not always, learn to exercise on its own. "Enough space" is room to spread and flap wings without hitting them on anything. Proper equipment includes swings, large branches extending over the cage, and toys hanging above the cage on which the bird can climb and flap.

While a sedentary bird that has been sitting and cuddling for a long time might, at first, resist exercise, the long-term benefits make a *gradually* increasing program well worth the effort.

Easy ways to inspire avian exercise:

• Provide a knotted, free-swinging rope or ring and bell toy for the bird to climb. The rings should be large enough to allow the bird's whole body to pass through or too small for the bird to insert its head.

• Play hide-and-seek and peek-a-boo around corners in unfamiliar territory; try to make the bird chase you to avoid being left alone in a strange place. It's not a good idea to encourage a bird, particularly a hand-fed bird, to roam around unsupervised.

• Play with the bird with a knotted rope, gently swinging the bird as it holds the rope with beak or claws (do this in an open area, so if the bird lets go it won't smash into something).

• Make the bird seek you out—including climbing up your body without assistance—if it wants to get off the floor.

• Parrot behavior consultant Sally Blanchard suggests playing "fetch" as you would with a dog. Entice the bird to return with the small bauble by saying "Good bird." Reward a successful fetch with further praise and petting.

• Sensitively loft the feather-trimmed bird onto the bed or sofa or to its cage so that it "flies" the last few feet.

• It is important that a parrot have a cage for numerous climbing opportunities rather than just a perch. (A perch is approximately 2 linear feet (60 cm) whereas a 2 foot by 2 foot by 2-foot (60 cm × 60 cm × 60-cm) cage is 40 square feet (3.7 m²) or 20 times more climbing space.)

• Provide a "climbing tree" or large natural branch. Put rings or grapes on the ends of all the twigs so that the bird has to climb around to eat or remove them.

Exercise is a simple cure for many parrot behavior problems. A bird that is just sitting around all day will improvise behaviors such as screaming and nipping, or might commence nesting behaviors such as sitting in the corner and chewing or laying eggs. Encouraging exercise can return a truculent teenager or mature bird back into the sweetly disposed animal you remember.

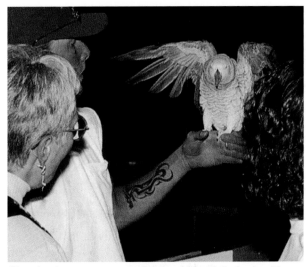

Flapping is a necessary and enjoyable activity for healthy companion parrots. (African grey parrot)

Toys!

Toys are absolutely necessary for good physical, emotional, and behavioral adjustment in a companion parrot. Avian expert and biologist Dr. Matthew Vriends reports that foraging for food consumes more than 90 percent of the wild parrot's daily activity. Try as we might, we can't replicate all elements of a wild environment. In captivity, providing food eliminates the need to forage, creating a need for other activities, and therefore toys.

Toys provide opportunities for decision making, intellectual development, physical exercise, the release of aggression, nurturing instincts, and other role-playing behaviors. From a feather or a sliver of wood used to scratch to a spoon for eating, birds love to use simple tools, and toys are simply tools for fun. A parrot that is not provided with toys will improvise makeshift toys out of its own feathers, slivers or chips of wood, food, cage parts, dishes, or any other environmental elements it can reach. A wise owner provides lots of safe-for-the-bird toys so that the bird does not injure itself or the environment by creating toys such as electrical cords, plants, furniture, walls, or other objects that have not been safety-tested for birds.

The activity provided by toys is essential for long life and good health. Avian interactions with toys also provide hours of happy entertainment for humans. A bird who has learned to play alone is a treasured companion indeed.

It's surprising how very often a parrot behavior consultant, when confronted with a two- or three-year-old bird who is biting out of control, hears the following story:

"Well, we gave him a toy once, when we first got him; but he didn't play with it, so we didn't give him another one."

With an examination of the bird's environment and a little prodding, the owners might remember that the bird responds to the telephone and the doorbell, opens the cage door, opens the food-service doors, swings on the door, bangs the carrying handle around on top of the cage, and makes soup in his water bowl with anything he can find. It is easy to figure out how the bird entertained itself. It had lots of toys; it just didn't have planned toys, commercially designed toys, or socially productive toys.

Stimulation provided by toys is particularly important during the developmental period called the "terrible two's." Toys reinforce good social development by providing opportunities for role playing, successful decision making, and distraction from socially unacceptable habits. Many birds "parent" their toys in much the same way as their owners "parent" them, scolding and punishing as well as soothing, feeding, and rewarding.

Quite a few commercial parrot toys are designed to simulate natural behavior. The Polly Dolly may be a parent-role toy consisting of cloth, string, leather, jute, wood, and a bell. It is an excellent stimulus for nurturing and "preening." This toy is an extremely beneficial distraction for feather chewers. Watch out for a bird

Play rings should be large enough to completely allow the birds to pass through or too small to allow the head entry. (blue and gold macaw)

with no other behavioral problems becoming overly attached, and therefore aggressive around the toy.

A young parrot in the developmental period should be given at least two new toys at a time. A mature companion parrot should have a minimum of one new indestructible or semi-destructible toy monthly. A healthy parrot requires many destructible toys monthly, and if they are not provided, they will be "found."

The cardboard rolls from inside paper towels are excellent chewables, as are clean, nontoxic bottle caps; but avoid excessive colored ink, staples, carbon and carbonless paper. The cardboard rolls may be cut into large cardboard "beads" and strung on rope or twine. These cardboard rolls can be punctured in numerous places and have short lengths of jute, twine, or shoelaces pulled through the holes and knotted. A nut or a few sunflower seeds might be placed inside a cardboard roll, which could then be closed at the ends with biodegradable tape. Punch a few holes in the cardboard so that the bird can see what's moving around inside, and Paco will spend much happy time removing the contents from inside the roll. Any of these paper products may contain toxic inks or glues, so watch to see if they wind up in the water bowl and eliminate them if the bird insists on soaking paper or cardboard remnants.

Cages are the gymnasium of companion parrots and climbing toys are their exercise equipment. Most parrot-type birds have an innate love

Provide frequent challenging physical activities to help keep your bird fit and healthy. (Jardine's parrot)

of swinging and should be offered at least one swing in their environment. Other favored climbing toys include knotted natural ropes, ladders, branches, chains, or anything hanging from a chain. When suspending hanging toys from the ceiling, it is advisable to provide some form of protection for the ceiling, perhaps a pizza pan with a hole drilled in the middle with the ceiling hook passing through the hole in the pizza pan.

I believe every physically and emotionally healthy parrot-type bird needs at least one hanging toy. When asked to identify the best all-around bird toy, I unhesitatingly recommend a contraption sometimes

Even simple toys like rolled or folded paper can provide hours of happy, quiet entertainment. (hyacinth macaw)

marketed under the name "Olympic Rings." It is a series of hanging, interlocking rings with a bell connected to the bottom.

The rings should be large enough to allow the bird to pass completely through them. They should be hung in or over the cage in a space large enough to allow the bird to hang onto the toy and flap. As the bird climbs in and around higher rings, the bell and the lower ring will jingle enticingly. Your bird will enjoy a lifetime of fun and physical exercise with this mini-gymnasium, and it will do so *without you*!

This particular toy comes in metal and bamboo versions. The bamboo version is inexpensive and is perfect for cockatiels, parakeets, lovebirds, lories, and other small hookbills. It will, of course, be destroyed periodi-

cally. The metal version of this toy is virtually indestructible. The bell must be replaced periodically, of course, as enterprising parrots feel obliged to remove the clapper. There are cockatiel/conure-sized versions of this toy as well as Amazon-sized Olympic Rings readily available in metal, but these are not quite large enough for a full-sized cockatoo or macaw. A wrought iron company or individual who makes security bars can custom-make this very important piece of equipment in sizes large enough and sturdy enough to accommodate the large hookbills.

Since most conscientious parrot owners keep their bird's wing feathers trimmed for safety purposes, this toy is a fun way for the bird to achieve the exercise necessary to keep physically fit. It will help to prevent the onset of noise and behavior problems in large and small parrots.

Watch out for hanging toys with rings that are large enough for the bird's head, but too small to allow the bird to withdraw the head easily.

Many birds also enjoy holding toys. One of the favorite toys of many large cockatoos is a metal spoon. Not only do these birds often learn to eat and drink with their spoon, but they just love to watch humans jump when they drop the spoon, making a loud noise.

Toys may be used for overt behavioral purposes. Holding toys are an excellent "distraction device" for birds with a fascination for buttons, jewelry, and eyeglasses. If the bird goes for bright items, look for a brightly colored holding toy. If the bird will play only with destructible holding toys, get destructible holding toys. Little wooden barbells, the fruit-juice colored wooden lollipops, and regular Tinkertoys are good for this. Greg Harrison and Chris Davis in their chapter on behavior modification in *Clinical Avian Medicine and Surgery* suggest that a favorite toy withheld during the day may help to distract a parrot from after-work screaming.

Many parrots are particularly fascinated with toys that have moving parts or make noise. The new lines of Plexiglas® toys with moving parts are exceptionally beautiful and durable. Kitchen measuring spoons that are linked together (metal or plastic) or old keys are suitable occasional or emergency toys (with supervision only), but these may present a hazard if the bird has a tendency to pry open the metal rings that attach them.

Puzzle toys must be taken apart to reach a reward such as a nut. Parrots love those wooden cages with almonds inside. Most types of parrots merely chew the bars away to get to the almonds. Occasionally, we hear of a quaker or cockatoo who manipulates the almonds out of the cage without chewing through the bars.

Food toys, including whole, hard nuts such as walnuts or Brazil nuts, are interesting and nourishing. Several lines of toys now incorporate nuts into their design. Interesting toys may be fabricated from coconuts, which are highly caloric and helpful in putting weight on a stubborn eater. Avoid fruits with pits such

Large parrots should not play with smaller parrots without very close supervision.

as cherry, peach, or avocado; they look like fun to play with, but some of them may be toxic.

Interactive toys: There are now available waterproof, electronic bird-activated music boxes. I believe we are just a few years away from bird-activated interactive speech training devices.

A parrot that has received no new environmental stimulation in quite some time may be reluctant to play with new toys. Inducing a parrot-type bird to play with toys can almost always be accomplished by stuffing the toys with paper towels or by tying knots of paper towels to the toys (leave the corners of the paper towels sticking out). Real paper towels or unprinted newsprint are the papers of choice for inducing chewing and playing.

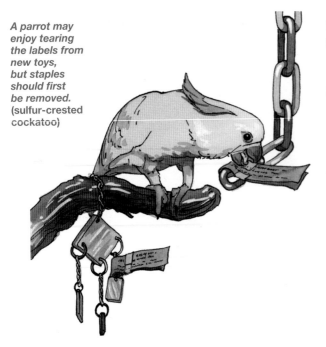

A parrot may enjoy tearing the labels from new toys, but staples should first be removed. (sulfur-crested cockatoo)

little brain wheels turning. "I've got to get this thing apart *right now!*"

Stimulating the Reluctant Talker

Different types of parrots are known to have differing propensities for mimicking human speech. The ease with which a parrot can physically produce speech is probably determined by the musculature in the trachea. Sound is produced by expelling air across the mouth of the bifurcated trachea. Variations in the sound are produced when the bird alters the "depth" and shape of the trachea. Some parrots such as the African grey parrot seem to have great ability to produce various sounds while others such as the cockatiel have limited ability to produce varied sounds. There is also great variation between individuals of the same type. A good-talking cockatiel might have a larger vocabulary than a poor-talking African grey.

A well-socialized, home-bred baby parrot often learns to talk more quickly than a human infant. It is somewhat more difficult to stimulate a wild-caught bird to learn to communicate verbally with human speech.

In addition to physical propensity, a parrot must be motivated to communicate. I believe parrots who rapidly narrow the pupil of their eyes ("pinpointing" or "flashing") are demonstrating a high level of interest in whatever is going on, including verbal communication. Frequent pinpointing is often

Care should be taken to ensure that the parrot is not ingesting pieces of toys or soaking them in the water bowl. Breakable and chewable inorganic toys are best provided only with supervision. Toys provided without human supervision should be unbreakable (metal or Plexiglas®, etc.). In particular, watch out for bells with lead clappers and holding or sitting-on-the-floor toys weighted with lead. No toy should be considered 100 percent safe. A really creative bird can make a hazard out of almost any toy.

A well-adjusted hookbill with a new toy is quite a sight. I always wonder what it thinks it is doing. The bird will grab the new toy and feverishly begin "working" it. You can almost see the

observed in good-talking parrots, and I believe lack of or infrequent pinpointing can be an indication of either poor health or a lack of curiosity.

Talking ability in parrots is unrelated to disposition. Some of the orneriest, meanest, most aggressive birds I have ever seen were great talkers. Many of the environmental manipulations we use to stimulate a reluctant talker are also those we use to reduce aggression. A balance must be maintained so that the bird is happy and excited about life, but not arrogant and temperamental enough to abuse humans.

Presuming a particular bird is of a type known to be capable of human speech, the following will help stimulate the nontalking parrot to speech.

• Include the bird in your daily rituals like showering, grooming (be careful with aerosols), and eating. Allow the bird to observe you sleeping and expressing affection. Participating in or observing these activities replicates the feeling of being a part of the flock and there will be a natural instinct to desire communication with other members of the flock.

• If the bird is usually housed lower than eye level and there is little problem with aggression, allow it to spend some social time in a very high place. The intoxication of height might stimulate aggression, screaming, or in a shy bird, speech.

• If the bird seems to suffer from poor "self-esteem" but is acclimated to the home environment, try allowing it a little more wing feather than

Yellow-naped and yellow-headed Amazons seldom need much stimulation to vocalize. (yellow-napped Amazon)

usual when grooming; or perhaps allow the wing feathers to grow in completely to stimulate the motivation to communicate.

• Model for the bird by calling back and forth with a human companion. Talk to the bird as you would to a human baby, using words to represent their meaning. Put a human companion in a competitive situation where the human companion receives a reward that the bird wants for speaking an easy-to-say word like "What."

• Try to provide a like-species role model to teach the bird to talk. If you can't find a role model, try establishing a rival or competitive student.

Although this spray would be too scary for many birds, this Green-cheeked Amazon loves it!

Magpie," or perform *Brigadoon* on Sunday mornings.

• Participate in passive games such as "blink" and "peep-eye" (see page 36).

• Most importantly, if there are several people in the household, *talk to each other* as well as to the bird.

Birds and Bathing

Bathing is an extremely pleasurable activity for birds. With the exception of the grey parrots, both African and Timneh, most common companion parrots take to it like the proverbial duck. Accompanied by comical postures and silly sounds, a spray bath may be the very first way a new owner/bird team can entertain friends and family.

Small parrots bathe readily in water dishes. Some parrots, like lories, literally bathe their water away several times a day and must be monitored frequently to guard against a dry water bowl (it is also helpful to provide a water tube for drinking). Gray-cheeked parakeets have even been known to cause their own screaming problems by bathing away their water, and then screaming their little blue heads off because there is nothing to drink. (In the presence of a screaming problem, check first to see if there is clean fresh water available.) Mid-sized and larger hookbills seem to prefer a fine spray-mist bath, which should be provided (except in extremely cold weather) a couple of times a week.

• Try to learn the meaning of a particular sound the bird uses; then use it with the same meaning.

• Try allowing access to a bird-safe "mirror"—a flat piece of shiny metal that swings on a chain. Watch out for the development of aggression around the bird mirror.

• Many birds find it fun to talk "into" the corner or the seed dish. Give the bird an interesting "resonating" toy in its cage, maybe a jar, metal can, or plastic cup.

• Watch lots of Tarzan movies and nature programs. Yell at television sports activities, in bird screams if possible.

• Stand out of sight of the bird and whistle. Try to get the bird to whistle back.

• Make up stories that mention the bird's name frequently. Sing to the bird when you run the shower, dishwasher, or vacuum cleaner.

• Establish singing, dancing, or music rituals: vacuum to "William Tell Overture," shower to "The Thieving

When introducing a new or reluctant parrot to spray baths, begin with a clean, new bottle filled with fresh tap water that has not been allowed to stand and grow dangerous microorganisms. Watch out for very hard water, overtreated water, or water suspected of harboring giardia. This little parasite is not unusual in mountain communities, particularly during spring runoff. It is a common cause of illness-related feather chewing and can kill both chicks and adult birds.

As with the introduction of new foods, a parrot may be reluctant to enjoy this new activity, but planning and persistence pay off. A hot sunny afternoon is ideal, as the bird will naturally wish to cool off. If the bird has never been sprayed, it is sometimes helpful to run the dishwasher, vacuum cleaner, hair dryer, or shower, as these sounds can help to stimulate the bird's desire to bathe. Set the nozzle for the finest possible mist, hold the bottle at least a foot away from the bird, lower than the bird, and spray a continuous mist above the bird's head so that water falls down on the bird like rain in the forest. It is sometimes helpful to make soothing, cooing noises when initiating a bird to the spray-mist bath. Amazons, cockatoos, and macaws may scream with delight and enjoy having accompaniment (you!) in their screaming.

An effectively bathed bird will look a little like a drowned rat. This may be difficult to accomplish on a healthy, dusty cockatoo that has not been bathed recently. Even a bird

Parrots are more likely to respond favorably to a spray bath if the spray bottle is held lower than the bird and the water falls down like rain from over the bird's head. (Amazon)

whose feathers are not repelling the water will require at least a couple of quarts of water for a good bath. If it is cold outside, be sure the room is at least 70–75°F (21–23.8°C). If tap water is extremely cold, the air will further cool it, so start with warm,

almost hot water. When it is cold outside, it may be best to bathe the bird in a warm bathroom, then blow dry with a hair dryer or direct a heat lamp toward the bird until it is *absolutely dry*. Many birds will respond to the hair dryer with exactly the same delight as the spray bath.

Because bathing is a community ritual for these flocking birds, behavioral benefits accrue from the sharing of a shower by bird and owner. I believe a new bird should first observe the owner sleeping (also a shared flock activity) and then see the owner eat and bathe to establish common (behavioral) ground upon which to build a relationship. Many caring owners include their parrots in their own daily grooming rituals, beginning with a shower. Provide a comfortable perch such as a wooden 2-by-2 on top of the shower door or perhaps a wooden dowel for the shower curtain. There are several manufactured shower perches available. While some birds actually like the water as it comes directly from the showerhead, I believe it is usually too strong and can drown the poor bird. An active shower with strong water pressure will deflect water off the human body onto the bird; but the spray bottle remains the safest, most effective way to include a parrot in human bathing rituals. Ideally, there will be much singing of duets.

If the owner bathes rather than showers, the spray bottle will be a necessary accessory for the bird's benefit. Then, of course, the bird must not be left unsupervised with a bathtub full of water or an uncovered toilet.

Showering with the bird by the less-than-favorite owner is an excellent way to work on the modification of overbonding. Even if you can't usually handle the bird, take the bird on a perch to the bathroom, share a shower and a song, and watch the relationship improve!

Letting the bird observe and groom during human grooming rituals—shaving, blowing hair dry, etc.—will further reinforce the "flocklikeness" of the parrot and its people. Aerosols such as deodorant and hair spray should be applied only after the bird has been removed from the area.

In addition to numerous behavioral advantages, bathing provides health benefits. Infrequently bathed birds have ratty-looking, sometimes tattered feathers. They may become feather chewers as a result of trying to groom dirty or brittle feathers. Bathing promotes tight, well-locked feathers and supple feather condition. In dry climates, infrequent spraying (along with a vitamin A deficiency) may contribute to the development of allergies, disease, or sinus problems.

Bathing is one of the easiest ways to improve the behavior of even poorly socialized birds. It is a basic avian need. Without the healthful recreational diversion of frequent drenching showers, a companion parrot may become a screamer, biter, or feather chewer; but probably Paco will merely be cranky and dirty.

Grooming the Bird for Safety

Just as failure to contain a dog or cat is the greatest cause of injury, loss, and death, failure to properly trim wing feathers is probably the greatest cause of injury, loss, and death to uncaged companion birds. But containment isn't the only reason to groom a bird. The periodic maintenance of wings, toenails, and beak is necessary for safe, successful living-room lifestyles.

Unfortunately, new bird owners sometimes mistakenly believe that wing clipping is an "inhumane" solution to dangers inside and outside the home. Probably the reverse is true. This simple, nonsurgical procedure resembles a haircut and must be repeated with similar frequency.

Some of the most heartbreaking injuries seen by avian veterinarians—fried, boiled, or outright burned pet birds—are the direct result of allowing free flight in the home. Death caused by startled birds flying into uncovered expanses of glass, mirror, or ceiling fans are totally preventable with periodic wing trims. Drowning—possibly the most frequent cause of death in the home—is prevented with wing trims combined with toilet bowl covering and the practice of not leaving sinks, tubs, pots, glasses, or containers of water or other liquids uncovered in the presence of unsupervised companion birds.

I believe companion animals are benefited by their association with humans. A domestic cat living wild

This baby grey parrot's wing feathers are barely trimmed to keep it out of trouble either by flying or falling.

has a life expectancy of less than a year but . . . an Amazon parrot that has a life expectancy of less than 10 years in the wild may live well past 50 in captivity. Appropriate and reasonable care favorably alter the companion animal's life expectancy. Timely wing feather trims are a big part of appropriate and reasonable care.

Since wing feathers do not grow continuously, they may be compared to human eyebrows. Growing to a certain length, they remain that length until they fall out and are replaced. Feathers remain the trimmed length until they fall out and are replaced by whole feathers. Timely regular clipping will not completely prevent a bird from flying. Wing trimming will, optimally, prevent boisterous flying in the house—like preventing children from running on a wet swimming pool sidewalk. A well-clipped pet bird retains balance and self-confidence while forfeiting the ability to gain altitude.

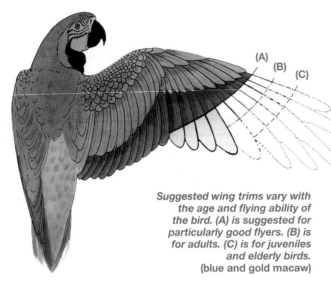

(A) (B) (C)

Suggested wing trims vary with the age and flying ability of the bird. (A) is suggested for particularly good flyers. (B) is for adults. (C) is for juveniles and elderly birds.
(blue and gold macaw)

The "utility clip" is probably the most dependable, widely-accepted clipping configuration. It involves the clipping of the first eight or nine primary flight feathers (ten long feathers on the ends of the wing that slant away from the body) just at the point where they are covered by the next layer of feathers.

A very light-bodied bird (cockatoo, cockatiel, parakeet, or dove) may require the trimming of all ten primaries and, perhaps, even a couple of the secondary flight feathers (ten lower inside wing feathers that slant toward the body) to restrict altitude.

Another popular clip is the "modified show" clip or "escape artist" clip, which leaves the two longest primary feathers and trims back the other eight flight feathers from there. This may be successfully employed only with heavy bodied birds like African

greys, some Amazons, and some macaws. It is not recommended by most professional groomers, who might be held liable if a treasured companion bird flew away.

The "escape artist" clip leaves those two long end feathers vulnerable to being caught in cage bars or knocked out. Birds regain flight capacity more quickly, sometimes when only one or two feathers regrow. This clip must be meticulously maintained—trimming new feathers as soon as they no longer have the retained sheath indicating blood supply. This clip is not at all dependable for a bird outside because the presence of wind and enough space to catch the wind is all that is needed for flight.

Visually check a bird perched on the hand by holding the foot and moving the hand down with just enough speed to require the spreading of wings. Clip regrowth as it appears. A functional test of flight ability may be made in a carpeted area by standing across the room from the cage and gently lofting the bird toward the cage. A flighted bird will usually elect to fly to the cage. A properly clipped bird may flutter to the floor.

Neither visual checks nor functional indoor tests can truly demonstrate that a bird cannot gain altitude. Outdoor excursions are always risky. A bird that is too lazy to fly across the room might be frightened enough to fly into a dog run or busy street in an uncontrolled outdoor setting. It can be a heartbreaking experience.

Untrimmed toenails can also be life threatening to a companion parrot. Because of the physical structure of the parrot's feet—with four toes, two opposing two—a parrot climbing on a wire cage must be able to stretch the foot completely open to "unhook" toenails from the pair of cage bars usually spanned by the foot. If the toenails become too long, the bird may not be able to open the foot wide enough to climb easily from place to place in the cage. If the bird is frightened it might merely break a leg; if it panics and cannot get loose from the bars, it might die. If it does not die from the stress of being caught on the cage bars, it might die of thirst because it cannot reach the water supply.

Sharp toenails are necessary in the wild where a fallen bird might be dinner; but in a companion parrot, they can negatively affect the human/avian relationship by causing pain to the handling humans. Unintentional reactions by humans to sharp toenails may cause biting by the bird, changing loyalties by the bird, or insecurity on the part of both humans and bird. The owner of a poorly groomed and poorly trained parrot may go to work on Monday looking like a weekend intravenous drug user or a victim of spouse abuse.

Most parrots must be restrained for nail grooming, but some parrots, particularly hand-fed parrots, initiated early to nail clipping as a part of social interaction, learn to allow nail grooming without restraint. This makes the whole process more enjoy-able for both humans and bird. But one of the most obvious behavioral advantages of grooming is that the parrot becomes used to the restraint. Not only is the occasionally restrained bird more cooperative overall (just as frequently groomed dogs are said to have better dispositions), the frequently groomed bird who is accustomed to restraint fares better during veterinary care when restraint stress might mean the difference between life and death. A thorough behavioral evaluation usually includes a description of "grooming stress" or lack thereof. Frequent grooming by the same handler reduces or almost totally eliminates grooming stress in most well-adjusted birds.

I see less towel fear with a towel that is approximately the color of the bird; but any neutral, solid color towel that is free of strings or loose threads will suffice as an appropriate restraint garment. Approach from the front, below the bird, holding one end of the towel in each hand with the middle of the towel drooping around the bird's breast. Completely, loosely envelop the bird in the towel, moving your less-dominant hand to the back of the bird's neck. Holding through the towel, grip the bird around the neck with the thumb and forefinger touching, or in the case of a very large bird, almost touching just below the bird's beak. Position the bird so that the towel may be opened from the front. Check to see that there is no pressure from the hand or towel on the bird's eyes. Check to see that the bird's breast is not restrained.

Because a parrot has no diaphragm, the chest must move in and out to draw air into the lungs and air sacs.

With the help of an assistant, you can either ball the foot and expose the toe and nail on the opposing side of the foot or gently pull the two opposing toes on one foot apart and clip the tip from the nail. Be careful to avoid the vein that supplies blood to the nail. In light-colored nails this can be seen easily with back light. It is more difficult with dark toenails. Bleeding is always a possibility. A dependable coagulant such as Kwik-Stop or silver nitrate should be readily available in the event of a bleeding toenail.

In an emergency one might cauterize the nail with a hot, recently blown-out match or a heated fork tine. Many professional groomers use a grinding tool such as a Dremel to reduce sharp toenails on medium and larger hookbills. While it is slightly more time-consuming than clipping the nails, there is less danger of bleeding. In addition, the ground toenail is immediately smooth and comfortable for the human hand. There is also a grooming tool that uses heat to melt or burn the nail back.

I believe most companion parrot relationships are best served by having a professional groomer, an outsider, perform regular maintenance on wing feathers, toenails, and beaks. This protects the sensitive, trusting relationship you have worked so hard to build.

Sometimes, however, with the more aggressive species such as Amazons and macaws, certain advantages accrue from having the best-loved human perform the grooming chores. If the bird is over-bonded to a particular person, either of two behaviorally desirable things might happen.

One, the bird might withdraw a little from the person to whom it is overbonded and cease attacking other household humans.

Or, two, the bird might decide it actually enjoys the grooming process, which could in itself strengthen the human/bird bond. I have seen quite a few conures and *Brotogeris* who loved to have the tip gently filed off the upper mandible with an emery board. This is the only nonprofessional form of beak grooming I advocate, for the stress involved in grinding a bird's beak can kill the bird. Most beak grooming should be done only by professionals. In particular, infrequently groomed birds (less than once a year) or birds in poor health should be groomed only by an experienced avian veterinarian. Watch the bird's response during grooming. Unless you are very faint of heart, don't let someone groom the bird outside your presence. If the bird hates the groomer or the groomer seems to handle the bird poorly, look for another groomer.

The Screaming Parrot

As previously discussed, the parrot is an aural creature, "prompting" parents to provide food and care by vocalizing even from within the egg. The parrot is also a very social creature. These natural tendencies combine to create the ability and desire to learn human speech. They are also responsible for the development of screaming behaviors.

Some loud vocalization is part of a parrot's natural expression, such as: "Wake up, it's morning!" "Everybody go to roost, it's getting dark!" "Here I am, I'm a cockatoo!" and "Sing along with me."

When evaluating a "screaming problem," begin with a diary to document the times, duration, and intensity of screaming. Some types of parrots have a greater tendency to scream, and some types have natural calls or "voices" that humans find annoying. It is probably easier for a person to endure 20 minutes of blue crown conure screaming than 10 minutes of Moluccan cockatoo screaming or even 5 minutes of Patagonian conure screaming. Usually, more than three to five minutes of screaming at a time more than five times a day (except for "singing" along with music or stimulating sounds like the shower) is unnatural for most species and problematic in human living situations.

Screaming is a learned behavior. It can be picked up from other birds, crying babies, or barking dogs. A parrot can teach itself to scream. This behavior is easily (usually unintentionally) reinforced by humans. Ignoring the behavior increases the calling response. Punishments

Some loud vocalizations can be expected, but "constant" screaming can signal something wrong in the environment. (blue-crowned mealy Amazons)

increase frustration levels and often exacerbate screaming. Screaming is best controlled with anticipation and prevention.

Hunger or thirst: Empty cups can easily contribute to the development of a screaming problem. Birds normally scream at feeding time. In the wild, loud calls accompany their arrival at foraging areas, inviting the flock to dine. A companion bird knows when it's time to eat; and if food or water isn't there, Paco will scream, "Where's dinner?"

Isolation: A bird that is isolated from flock, family, or mate will call out for its buddies. Visual isolation as well as actual physical isolation can stimulate speech and/or screaming. Talking or soft whistling back and forth with the bird will model the desired response. A screaming bird can sometimes be placated with the addition of well situated mirrors so that human companions are visible around that kitchen or living room corner.

Boredom: Parrots are extremely intelligent. In addition to toys of *their* choice, they need visual stimulation. Sight is their most highly developed sense, and television is the easiest way to entertain a lonely parrot. A bird sitting at home all day is resting up for play time. Just when Mom or Dad needs rest, Paco is ready for fun and games. A television on a timer set to come on a few hours before the humans get home will use some of that pent-up bird energy. Never forget or underestimate a parrot's attraction to squealing and flashing lights and bells.

Eating and the related "foraging" (digging through the bowl, tonguing things) are excellent distractions from screaming related to boredom. Withhold food from the bird for a few hours, then place an interesting and diverse assortment of food in the bowl just *before* the bird would usually begin to scream.

Lack of exercise: A healthy parrot has lots of energy. If there is no provision for flapping, screaming or feather chewing can take its place. To encourage flapping, provide climbing and swinging toys; or place the wing-trimmed bird on the hand then move the hand down quickly so that the bird flaps its wings; or swing the bird on a knotted rope (sensitively, of course) until it is breathing heavier. A sedentary parrot beginning an exercise program may become winded in only a few seconds, but exercise time can be gradually increased. If the bird is mature and has had neither exercise nor a vet check for some time, a visit to an avian veterinarian should be made before beginning an exercise program for the control of screaming.

Bathing is a logical follow-up to aerobics. A fine-mist shower sprayed from below to fall down on the bird is a fitting reward for exercise. Many parrots will continue flapping and having "silly attacks" during a spray bath.*

A bird that is busy "zipping" wet feathers (preening) after a bath is not screaming.

Pressure to breed: A bird with out-of-control hormones may call incessantly for a nonexistent mate. Some of this may be seasonal; some may be modified with diet. Aviculturists have long understood that birds may be stimulated to breed with the addition of animal protein, specifically eggs, to the diet. I believe I see increased aggression and screaming in companion parrots with diets including more than 18 percent protein, particularly if the primary source of that protein is eggs. If you don't want your bird to exhibit breeding behavior, avoiding feeding eggs. Try substituting small amounts of cheese, tofu, or tuna for daily protein.

There are *many* other reasons for screaming and many other techniques to modify screaming. Some causes are easy to figure out; some

---

*I believe it is dangerous and confusing to spray a stream of water as a punishment. Bathing should be a welcome reward. A bird that is punished with water can develop other neurotic behaviors such as feather chewing and foul temper.

are very subtle. A parrot behavior consultant may be able to tell to what extent screaming can be modified in a particular bird by evaluating the home environment, taking a detailed history, manipulating and reevaluating the environment. Don't give up! It might take more than one try, but the peace is well worthwhile!

Feather Destructive Behavior

As a veteran fingernail biter for well over 40 years, I can relate to the feather-chewing bird. Like nail biting in humans, feather chewing is an enigmatic problem that may resolve itself seemingly spontaneously or never correct at all. Usually, however, behavioral feather chewing or self-mutilation can be at least partially or seasonally corrected with the help of a behavioral history, environmental manipulations, improved training, and distraction from the vice.

Begin with a trip to an avian veterinarian. The chewing of feathers may arise from disease processes or nutritional deficiency, and the possibility of a physical problem is ever present. While feather chewing that is related to the desire to breed is technically a hormonal problem, or rather related to stress generated by hormone activity, it can often be successfully treated with behavioral techniques. Even though feather chewing in many individual birds may be traced to a physical or dis-ease origin, I believe that most feather chewing in healthy birds will respond once the physical problem is remedied if sound behavioral modifications are begun promptly at the onset of the problem.

While it is not unusual for a normal healthy parrot to pluck out a feather or two, particularly during molting, a self-mutilating bird might remove all breast, primary wing, or tail feathers in one sitting before proceeding to damage the skin. The surprised owner sometimes returns to the room to find a bare-breasted bird and a pile of feathers on the floor or bottom of the cage. I once saw a Goffin's cockatoo chew off every breast feather in 20 minutes when a noisy Patagonian conure was introduced two rooms away in a very large house.

It is generally agreed that behavioral chewing of feathers probably arises from some form of stress. The stress may be caused by worn, injured, or damaged feathers; incomplete molt; improper cage, height, or location; diet; handling patterns; bathing patterns; inappropriate light periods; lack of physical or mental stimulation; isolation; or temporary or permanent loss of an owner (abandonment). If the source of the stress can be identified and removed quickly, the problem usually resolves itself spontaneously. For example, a parrot may chew its feathers every year when it is left behind for the family vacation and discontinue chewing when the family returns.

Once feather chewing appears, immediate steps must be taken to

Even this parrot may be able to overcome feather destructive behavior with work on health, diet, and/or environment. (green-winged macaw)

ensure that this stress reaction does not become habitual. Long-term feather chewing can damage feather follicles beyond their ability to regrow healthy feathers. The longer feather chewing continues, the more difficult it is to break. At this point the behavior is defined as a "vice," an ongoing fault. As a vice, it can easily be learned from one bird by another; indeed this is one of the hazards of boarding birds. I once saw a beautiful blue-and-gold macaw—who was, of course, also feeling abandoned—learn feather chewing from an African grey in the next cage while being boarded in a veterinary clinic.

Begin the quest for a fully feathered parrot by taking a behavioral history. When was the onset of the chewing behavior? Was there some environmental change at that time? Was the bird appropriately caged? Was the bird trained to step up or socialized not to scream, bite, or chew? Was the bird provided with opportunities to make choices? Was

the bird deprived of sleep? Deprived of interesting things to see, hear, and touch? Was the bird receiving a balanced diet? Was a child or another animal introduced to the home? Was the cage moved? Was the bird neglected or abandoned? Was the bird receiving too little or too much of some important nutrient such as protein?

Seasoned aviculturists have observed that the onset of feather destruction not infrequently accompanies a late or incomplete molt. Parrot behavior consultants such as Sally Blanchard, working as I do in the "laboratory" of the living room, have observed captive-raised babies begin feather chewing with damaged wing or tail feathers. These damaged feathers try to grow in but are repeatedly broken or chewed off. The source of these damaged feathers might be simple baby clumsiness; the chewing habit can be easily reinforced by lack of stimulation during the developmental period. A baby parrot with many broken wing and tail feathers, who is repeatedly breaking blood feathers, and "whining" or complaining, chewing the affected area, should see an avian veterinarian immediately lest the practice become an established pattern.

Real or perceived abandonment frequently coincides with the onset of feather chewing. Self-mutilating behavior can often be traced directly to a family vacation, the return of an owner to work, change of ownership, or death of an owner. The very best way to prevent the onset of this behavior from these sources is proper socialization. The bird should not be encouraged to overbond to one person, but rather be provided with many opportunities for interactions and relationships with various humans. A conscious effort should be made to teach the bird to entertain itself.

Prepare a companion parrot for an owner's return to work by increasing quality time, perhaps sharing music, morning showers, grooming rituals, or exercise followed by short but gradually increased periods of isolation. A bathed and well-exercised bird will contentedly groom for a while, eat, and nap. If the bird is to be left alone all day, quality visual and sound stimulation can be provided with a television on a timer, set to come on a few hours before the owner returns from work. A television left on all day will interfere with the bird's nap time and desensitize the bird to the stimulation it provides. A few hours of game shows just before the owner returns home will also help to curb screaming

Packing the Cage

Presuming that the bird is in a cage it likes, in a location it likes; presuming that diet and exercise are adequate; presuming that there is no teasing by human or animal companions, the bird may often be distracted from habitual feather chewing by *"packing"* the cage.

Completely fill the cage with clean branches that have not been sprayed with either insecticides or herbicides. There should be so little space left in the cage that the poor bird can barely stand up completely straight or turn around without coming into contact with branches. The branches should be small enough so that the bird can easily chew them out of the way to make a space for its own body. They should have bark that can be removed as a form of entertainment by the bird. We are trying to distract the bird from the habit of feather chewing long enough to learn the more natural parrot behavior of "making toothpicks."

If the bird seems extremely stressed by even the slightest change in the environment, pack the cage gradually—a branch or two every day for a period of a week or two. If the bird continues chewing on feathers, let the "bird-carved" space remain. Continue to provide lots of fresh new twigs in an easily accessible place.

and attention-demanding behavior immediately after work. Of course the bird should have ample space. A bird

In extreme cases, a collar may be necessary to prevent the progression of mutilation behaviors. (African grey parrot)

that spends all day in a cage needs a larger cage than a bird who does nothing but sleep in its cage. A parrot housed only on an open perch without the security or climbing opportunities provided by a cage can easily develop feather chewing as well as several other problem behaviors.

An emotionally healthy parrot should have access to several toys, thereby providing opportunities for decision making. "Shall I go climbing now or play with my bell?" Having access to several behaviorally acceptable choices gives a companion parrot a greater sense of control and, therefore, security.

The vacation feather chewer may be corrected by taking the bird on vacation, improving the technique of the in-home bird sitter, or by preconditioning for separation from owners with short visits to the location of the bird sitter. Not only should the bird sitter be experienced in the physical care of parrots, but also try to find a sitter that the bird likes.

Effective rebonding to a new owner is crucial in correcting the "abandoned" feather-chewing parrot. After at least two weeks of shared quality time spent feeding from the hand, bathing, eating, and sleeping in each other's presence, the bird should be taken on safe social outings where the new owner is the only familiar human. The new owner should take the bird to the groomer and the veterinarian, "rescuing" the bird from these frightening situations followed by rewards of cuddles (if the bird likes cuddles) or favorite foods.

Purely behavioral feather chewing in young birds: Stress caused by failure of independence, constant reprimands, lack of access to acceptable choices of behaviors, lack of understanding of what is expected, or understimulation during what should be an exciting, experimental time for the young parrot can easily lead to a life of chronic feather chewing. Early onset feather chewing can be difficult to correct, particularly if it has gone unchecked for many years. The remedy is to try to lead the bird through the period again modeling play behavior, and encouraging the development of play and other independent activities. This must be done slowly and sensitively, particularly if the bird is over eight years old.

I am not an advocate of collars for the modification of behavioral feather chewing. If the bird is a new chewer, the stressing situation may not yet have been resolved and the additional stress added by the collar can increase the desire to chew or cause the bird to become ill. Collars may be necessary when treating self-mutilation involving damaging skin and flesh.

Some birds enjoy "shredding" cotton or jute fibers. If a love for the disintegration of fabric is observed, provide a hankie or piece of fabric or two. It is always more effective if the bird is able to choose this object from a number of options that the bird itself discovers. For example, you might notice that Cecilia is crazy about that lavender bandana, so why not just donate it to the Cecilia cause. Monitor the bird initially to determine whether it is ingesting fibers, and be ever alert for really stringy fabric shedding threads that might entrap little toes and toenails.

I like Booda Bones and, of course, the personal parrot favorite, shoelaces. There is no more enticing object to a parrot than the tip end of a shoelace. I believe that many feather-chewing birds could be quickly and completely rehabilitated if we could just afford to pack their cages daily with new shoelaces.

South American parrots eat mineral-rich clay on a daily basis. Natives report that the birds are easier to catch if deprived of this mineral source for a few days.

Timing, too, can work for or against the recovering feather chewer. I believe the very best time to begin to rehabilitate the behavioral chewer is springtime. Summer, the molting season, is the time of most rapid feather growth, and the owner's ability to see progress will serve to motivate continued efforts. A regrowing program begun in April will often yield a feathered bird by September. A recovering feather chewer may relapse occasionally, but time between incidents will become longer as the behavior is discontinued.

Reading Parrot Body Language

Because it is difficult to read a bird's facial expressions, observers of parrot behavior look for body language to evaluate how a parrot feels. A lethargic bird with puffed-up feathers is probably not feeling well. Recognizing a sick bird has often been described in other books, but here we will discuss how parrots communicate normal, healthy emotions. Sensitive owners observing wagging or flaring tails, flipping wings, wiggling tongues, tapping feet, and pinpointing eyes are reading signals about what their bird is feeling.

Tail Wagging

A wagging tail might be saying, "I'm glad to see you!"; "That was interesting!"; or "My tail feathers are out of place!"

This behavior is usually performed with exuberance and frequently follows a "puff up and head shake"— the mannerisms that are used for greeting a beloved friend entering the area.

Wagging the tail rapidly back and forth is common in many types of

unhappy individual might occasionally express a nervous giggle. This behavior, like any other, must be evaluated within the context of all the bird's behavior.

When called for an evaluation, one of the things I look for is the presence or absence of tail wagging. In a previously unhandled bird (import or parent-raised domestic) the appearance of at least one or two tail wags during the first 20 minutes of observation by a stranger in their territory can evidence developing satisfactory adjustment to the home.

A companion parrot behavior consultant might begin a house call with a 20- to 40-minute observation and evaluation of the animal's behavioral adjustment to the environment. A second similar time period involves handling the bird to observe responses to stimuli and "training" to unfamiliar techniques to demonstrate what the bird is capable of. Finally, humans must be taught to perform the techniques and to reinforce acceptable responses.

During phase two of this process, I periodically place the bird on a perch, then sit lower than the bird and outside its personal space, watching for those tail wags. If I see a tail wag immediately or within the first 60 seconds after the bird has been handled, I know I can push the bird at least as far as it has been pushed, perhaps further. If the tail wag occurs one to two minutes after the bird is placed on the perch, I know that I should push no further. If there is no tail wag or if the tail wag

birds, including parrot-type birds. Some of the most frequent and vigorous tail waggers in the avian family are ducks and geese—water fowl— suggesting that perhaps the source of this behavior is shaking water from the tail. In the case of parrots, it is also observed in wet birds shaking water off their tails, as well as dry birds "shaking off" the remnants of their most recent experience.

The wag is usually described as a "termination behavior," which often occurs at the perceived end of one activity or the beginning of another. In my observation, in order for a tail wag to occur in a parrot, the experience must be at least tolerable and probably perceived by the bird as pleasant.

A tail wag is also something like a giggle. Although it might be occasionally absent in a happy creature, it is often absent in an unhappy one. Tail wagging is no guarantee of happiness and health, for even a sick,

comes more than two minutes after placing the bird on the neutral perch, I presume I have pushed too hard, and I must back off a little the next time I handle the bird or change my approach entirely.

Several behavior problems I see in companion birds may be related to malaise or depression. Increasing tail wags, puff outs, and pinpointing are indications of developing success when treating such conditions as anorexia, overweight, inactivity, and failure to talk.

If we start by manipulating only the environment until we are seeing more tail wags, particularly if they are accompanied by decreasing wing flips, we are probably progressing—however imperceptibly to the casual observer—toward a happier, better socialized hookbill. We're talking "baby steps" here, but every journey begins with the first step.

Stretching

Although I agree with some people who believe that kitties invented yoga, there is no question in my mind that birds invented tai chi, the Chinese system of calisthenics and meditation practiced to produce body flexibility and peace of mind.

Most healthy parrots practice a series of gracefully choreographed stretching motions frequently. The shoulders might be raised in unison, followed by the mirror image motion of extending the other wing and foot in unison. The message communicated by a bird's stretching like this is one of well-being. The stretch is a greeting or "initiation behavior" that usually comes at the beginning of the day or the beginning of the time of day that a bird interacts with human comrades. It is most often observed when people first enter the room.

The stretch says, "See how glad I am to see you?" An appropriate response is to mimic the bird (if the bird doesn't understand your words yet) or to reply with "Yes, you are very, very pretty, and I am very glad to see you, too."

Preening

The tiny little barbs on the feather filaments resemble the teeth of a zipper. A clean, healthy-looking feather is perfectly zipped. A physically and emotionally healthy bird spends a good deal of time keeping those feathers properly zipped. Preening, or grooming the feathers, expresses a sense of safety and well-being; but more, it expresses the feeling: "I want to look nice for you." A bird preening while sitting on a hand could be a prelude to greater expressions of bonded interest from the bird.

A healthy parrot preens its feathers often to keep them smooth and shiny. (Senegal parrot)

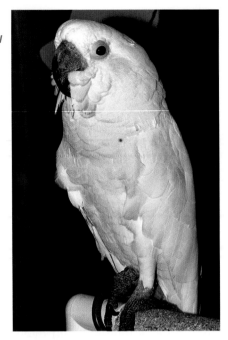

Facial feathers fanned over beak may signal contentment in cockatoos. (umbrella cockatoo)

Allopreening

When a bird feels compelled to preen human hair (head, facial, or otherwise) this is saying, "I like you; I want to help you look healthy and pretty for me." The appearance of alopreening from bird to human can signify a positive step toward an improved relationship.

A bird with a neck full of pin feathers with no avian companion to clean them off will depend on its human companion to remove the casing from pin feathers that it cannot reach itself. Instructions for this activity are found in How to Pet a Parrot, page 39.

Bird Scratching Its Own Head, Chin, or Neck

A bird with a dazed, come-hither look who has head and neck feath-

ers puffed up and is slowly scratching its own neck, chin, or head is saying "I'm so pitiful and lonely, I have to scratch my own self." This is clearly an invitation to pet: "Oh, Mom/Dad, won't you pleeeeease come scratch my head?"

Facial Feathers Fluffed Over Beak

In the presence of other aggressive signals, fluffed facial feathers might mean aggression; but within a peaceful context, face feathers fluffed over the beak are usually an extremely coy expression. This is particularly true when combined with self-scratching.

This behavior is frequently practiced by cockatoos who are saying, "I'm so sweet, I don't even have a beak."

I have seen a few cantankerous birds who will entice an unsuspecting stranger with this compelling look, and then bite them. Some of these creatures are little "con artists." If the human companion says, "Don't believe the look, the bird's a vampire!" it is probably safest to believe the human companion. I have, however, occasionally encountered birds that hated the owner and bit the owner whenever possible, but loved everybody else. This situation is even more unhealthy than a bird that bites everyone but the owner.

Beak Grinding

This behavior says, "I'm going to sleep now." A normal, healthy hookbill rubs the lower mandible against the inside of the upper mandible, eyes closing, standing on one foot. I believe this is a grooming activity that keeps the bird's lower beak sharp and ready to eat upon waking. A bird that has been very depressed for a long time might omit this behavior, with subsequent overgrowth of the lower mandible. This condition might also be accompanied by ill health. The sudden appearance of an overgrown beak is certainly a reason for a veterinary consultation, followed by a behavioral consultation if no health problems are found by the avian veterinarian.

Sleeping on One Foot

While this is a healthy behavior, suddenly noticing that the bird is spending a lot of time on one foot might mean that the bird is sleeping more than usual, which might indicate ill health.

Wing Flipping

I also look for flipping or slapping wings against the body when evaluating parrot behavioral adjustment. Wings might be flipping in anger, frustration, or because a feather is out of place. The bird might be in pain, or it might be settling down for sleep. A bird that is flipping its wings is not seeking interaction and may be threatening impending aggression. Many wing flips may indicate masturbation or sexual motivation.

A parrot that has flipped one wing once has said, "Watch it, I'm not sure I'm ready for this." A parrot that has flipped each wing once has said, "I'm

really quite over this." A parrot that has flipped both wings more than twice is either in pain or very agitated: "If you mess with me, you'll be sorry!" If the bird is large and the behavior is accompanied with pinpointing eyes or a flaring tail it is absolutely unwise to handle the bird at this time.

If most conditions are adequate, I think a companion bird with a frequent hostile, wing-flipping attitude, particularly when accompanied with flashing eyes, fanning tail, and in some cases a strong "parrot musk" odor probably needs more baths. Call it a "cold shower" or call it "raining in the jungle"; frequent animosity even passively expressed against peaceful companions is often accompanied by aggression and is unnecessary and unacceptable. If the angry, hostile, wing-flipping bird's environment, diet, and social patterns seem adequate, the bird may need more outlets to express energy. That might mean exercise or baths. The energy required to recover from a drenching rain shower probably prevents much non-food-related aggression both in the jungle and in the living room.

Just as I count increasing tail wags as an indication of approaching success when treating depression-related behaviors, I count decreasing wing flipping as an indication of developing success when treating established aggression in a companion hookbill.

Whether a parrot is sedentary or aggressive, the frequency of these two behaviors can be an indication of regression or progress toward

Pinpointing eyes, extended shoulders, and flared tails can indicate interest or aggression. (brown-headed and Senegal parrot)

Pinpointing

The narrowing of the pupil and enlargement of the iris—sometimes called "flashing"—is easily seen in a light-eyed parrot. This behavior, which is probably present but difficult to observe in dark-eyed birds, is frequently observed in species known for facility in acquiring human speech—grays, Amazons, conures, and macaws. While it is not unusual to see a parrot that pinpoints but does not talk, with the exception of dark-eyed birds, I have never taken a history of a parrot-type bird that talks that does not also exhibit an observable iris movement.

If we are trying to teach new words, the appearance of flashing eyes is a sign that this is an excellent time to model the words we want the bird to learn. But pinpointing is probably more an indication of motivation than an indication of talking ability.

Pinpointing is sometimes an indication of motivation to violence and frequently accompanies the flaring tail and stiffly extended shoulders of the courtship display. If we are unfamiliar with the bird or know or suspect that the bird has an uneven disposition, this is an excellent time to allow the bird some personal space.

behavioral goals. If we observe more wing flips than tail wags every day, we may be seeing a bird that is not happy in its environment, and the bird's human companions probably have justifiable reason to be less than thrilled with the bird's behavior.

Tongue Wiggling

This is most frequently and obviously observed in cockatoos and cockatiels, but is also seen in other types of parrots. Some people call this "beak chattering." It involves holding the upper and lower mandibles slightly apart and moving them up and down very quickly, combined with an apparent movement of the tongue in and out in a sort of "licking" or "tasting" motion. This behavior is probably translatable as "YumYumYumYum."

In human terms this is an expression of affection: "I like it!" or "I like you!"

This behavior is frequently accompanied by a fluff out and tail wag.

Flaring Tails

Unlike the pinpointing of eyes that may occur at moments of "normal" excitement, flaring tails demand ultimate respect. A flaring tail is a sign of exceptional excitement—such as sexual excitement—that is often accompanied by aggression. While one might continue to handle a well-known bird with pinpointing eyes, even a familiar bird may be on the verge of expressing aggression when a flaring tail accompanies the pinpoint eyes.

Begging

A parrot that is staring intently (at someone or something) with its body flattened out, with quivering wings held out at the shoulders, is saying "Gimme!" This is the same behavior in parrots as the classic begging behavior in dogs: standing on hind legs, front paws folded to chest. It is similar to the invitation-to-breed/solicitation stance in female parrots; but begging is usually more animated and less strident.

Misinterpreted Messages

Most parrots cannot verbally communicate their feelings to humans. They must rely on body language to tell us how they feel. Parrot behaviors are frequently misunderstood by new owners who are unaccustomed to their ways. I have seen many otherwise caring humans try to stop their birds from vocalizing normal exuberant parrot song. I have seen humans punish their birds for trying to talk during periods in which they were also trying to teach talking. Parrots have no vocal cords; they must practice making different sounds. Some parrots practice new sounds softly; some birds really blurt them out. Parrots are vocal. If all the bird's needs are being met, the sounds we are hearing are

A well-bonded grey parrot might solicit for food, toys, or attention. (African grey parrot)

probably expressions of delight and appreciation.

I have also seen quite a few new owners say that their bird "acted aggressive" when they tried to give it a spray bath. Often, when we reenacted the spray-bath scenario, we saw a normal, happy bird exuberantly enjoying the water.

I believe miscommunication between humans and their avian companions directly contributes to many parrot "behavior problems." If there is behavioral maladjustment in a parrot, the solution is often found in enhancing human ability to understand the bird.

Defending Territory

No companion animal seems more aggressive than a parrot who loves too much. Whether the bird is overbonded to a cage (location) or a person (perceived mate), intruders are chased rudely away. Even some of the smallest hookbills can scare an intruding human half to death.

A parrot may be "territorially overbonded" to a location, cage, or person; or may be "sexually overbonded" to a human who is a perceived mate. Both behavior patterns may be seasonal, but the former is present in both young and mature birds, while the latter is seen in mature birds. The ability to modify the behaviors depends upon the age and history of the bird and the sensitivity and cooperative skills of human companions.

Suppose your true love purchased for you the ultimate gift: a beautiful, outrageously expensive parrot that bubbled with enthusiasm whenever you talked and apparently wished for nothing more than to live and be loved by you. But within a few months, the bird was lunging angrily when you walked by and was infatuated with your significant other. Within another few months, it seemed that the bird wanted to either kill you or drive you out of your own home. This kind of "love triangle" can be emotionally devastating to even the strongest individual.

To overcome bonding-related aggression, one must first determine whether the bird is acting out of territorialism or sexuality. Many territorially motivated behaviors are similar to sexually motivated behaviors, although the former are substantially easier to modify.

If the behaviors are territorial, even though the bird will obviously cling to and protect *one* chosen person, there will be no history of regurgitation for only the chosen human (many baby parrots try to feed each other), no *excessive* wood chewing, and (in the case of Amazons and macaws, in particular) no strong "parrot musk" smell associated with a mature parrot in sexual overload. There will usually be tail displays and pinpointing of eyes. There may be attacks upon everyone except the favored human, with particular ferocity toward the human mate of the bird's perceived human "territory."

While it is difficult not to "flirt" with a talking, eye-flashing, and tail-displaying parrot, these behaviors should not be reinforced. In particular, no matter how funny it is to see a little bird terrorize a grown human, we must never laugh when Paco tries to kill our better half. This is surely a form of "spouse abuse" that reinforces the bird to attack.

We know that the smaller the territory over which the bird has control, the more intense the efforts to control that territory. This concept also applies to people. Generally speaking, the fewer people with whom the parrot interacts, the more passionately the bird will try to control this "human territory" by fending off intruders. In a family of five, the parrot might not let the spouse into the kitchen. In a family of two, the parrot might try to kill the spouse whenever it has the chance.

Treating territorial overbonding involves establishing a "commuter" lifestyle for the bird by removing the cage to an unfamiliar area in the home (making that area into a "roosting area") and providing a portable play area or basket with an appropriately perch-sized handle, so that the bird may have a moving "foraging area." Several play areas in various parts of the house can be provided with the use of unpainted baskets with handles (wrap the basket handle with jute or heavy twine for durability). If there are other pets in the house, it might be a good idea to hang the baskets from the ceiling. Of course, each "foraging area" should be outfitted with toys, food, and water dishes.

The companion parrot's behavior is improved by outings into unfamiliar territory: visits to the vet, a friend's house, a friendly pet store, or public event. Be sure to use dominance-prevention techniques such as retaining the bird on the hand or handling the bird with a towel and with handheld perches. Although a typical parrot *will* develop aggressive behavior solely as a result of being allowed to "hang out" on the favorite human shoulder, most parrots will not display aggressive behavior only as a result of being on the shoulder in *unfamiliar territory*. Visits to strange places improve the bond between the bird and *any* familiar human—particularly the perceived rival.

If aggressive parrot behavior is truly the result of sexual overload, treatment is more complicated, as we will discuss later. Early prevention training is necessary for good social adjustment in mature birds. I believe the chances of favorably modifying aggressive behavior resulting from

territorialism in a young parrot are very good, probably better than 95 percent. Modifying true sexually motivated aggression in most hookbills between 8 and 30 years old is more difficult, but may be accomplished much of the time if adequate early training has been provided. The bird may not be handleable during its breeding season, but will be fine the rest of the year.

An incident of violent aggression by a usually sweet bird exhibiting the above behaviors should be "charted" on a calendar. The aggressive behavior may recur on exactly the same date every year. I suggest special handling a week or two before the previously documented incident and a week or two after it during the reproductive years. During periods of peak hormonal activity in a large hookbill's teens and twenties, it is safest to handle the bird when you are wearing eyeglasses and using a hand-held perch.

A parrot allowed on the shoulder may sometimes express displaced aggression against a human face. (green-cheeked Amazon parrot)

An excited or "wound up" parrot might bite unpredictably. (sulphur crested cockatoo)

neously in a bird that has never before demonstrated aggression against the primary person.

Displaced aggression escalates with sexual maturity. If the bird attacks everyone but the primary person, someday it will attack the primary person. Displaced aggression toward the primary person is often more violent than any previous incident of overt aggression toward others.

"Passive" aggression: Many mature parrots will sweetly entice a human with song, words, and gestures, and then bite when approached. If you see a strange parrot begging for your attention, but are told "Don't you believe it," trust the people who are warning you.

Controlling overbonding: I believe many people obtain a parrot because they have a need to fill in their own emotional lives. I see women obtain a precious parrot when they lose a lover; I see men with new baby hookbills when their wives are nursing and bonding with human infants. But allowing a bird to become overbonded to only one person in a multiple-person household can be dangerous. Family members must coordinate their efforts to have a well-socialized bird that does not "pick on" anyone in the family. Use of the techniques described here will provide groundwork for a lifetime of successful social interaction with a companion parrot.

Height: A parrot that is housed too high may develop aggressive tendencies toward perceived "underlings." I have seen vicious Amazons

Overt aggression: Given the opportunity, a parrot will often attack the "other mate" of their very favorite person, that person's friends, children, or other pets.

Displaced aggression: Sometimes, however, a parrot bites not because it dislikes the object of the bite, but because it likes that person too much. The best-loved person is very often the victim of displaced aggression. Parrots seem to subscribe to the concept: "When you're not near the one you want to bite, bite the one you're near." I have seen many severe human facial injuries that were the result of having a beloved companion parrot on the shoulder when a spouse walked into the room or when attention was paid to another parrot. Be ever watchful. This behavior may emerge sponta-

turned into baby dolls by cutting only 5 or 6 inches (12–15 cm) off their cage stand. Height factors may be particularly problematic in macaws. I receive many calls from people with toddlers and maturing juvenile macaws. I often go to the home to find a bird on top of a cage at a height that causes it to look up at the male companion and down at the woman and children. With a young macaw, if we can either lower the bird or raise the height of the wife and children, the behavior is often *instantly* corrected and can be permanently reinforced by use of the other techniques discussed in this chapter.

Commuting: A parrot's indulgence in territorialism may be modified by providing the bird with a commuter lifestyle. Parrots who stay in exactly the same place all the time often become temperamental and "bity" (that's about a half-a-mile past "nippy" and means that the bird is doing actual physical damage to human flesh). African greys and cockatoos have very strong tendencies to become overbonded to the cage, expressing either aggression or fear when anyone approaches the cage.

In the wild, except when nesting, most parrots probably sleep in *approximately* the same place every night then go away every day to forage in many places. Strong aggressive tendencies probably do not develop to as great an extent in the foraging territories as in the roosting territory.

I believe a pet bird is best allowed to roost in a cage in a fairly isolated part of the home at night, then be included in family activities at many communal "foraging" or play areas during the day. The bird becomes dependent upon a person who physically takes it from the roost to the foraging areas. It is the task of the "less-liked" person to take the bird to "forage" every day. If the bird does not tolerate handling by this less-liked person, it is deprived of social interaction with the flock. The intelligent, manipulative parrot soon learns that social interaction with the less-liked person is necessary to get to the ones with whom it wants to be. The bird learns to enjoy social interaction with more humans.

I suspect that this transportation dependence is what parrot behaviorist Sally Blanchard is accomplishing with her training principle of never allowing the bird to climb out of the cage on its own. Although I have not heard that she advocates "roosting and foraging" in the manner recommended here, she develops the same dependency relationship by allowing the bird to leave the cage only on the human hand.

Outings: Outings into unfamiliar territory with less-than-favorite humans are particularly effective in the modification of aggression. A bird in a strange place in the company of strangers will most likely be very nice to any familiar person — even its most-hated rival. Social outings for parrots teach the bird that even when it is not in total control of the

Several aspects of companion parrot behavior may be improved by safe outings into unfamiliar territory. (blue and gold macaw)

environment, life is safe and stimulating and the less-than-favored person becomes a soulmate. A parrot who goes on lots of outings will be sweeter and better adjusted at home as well as in public. Watch for signs of stress, and avoid allowing the bird on the shoulder in the car, as unexpected behaviors can cause accidents. Some people allow the bird to sit on a small cage, perch, or basket and look out the window. The safest transportation is in a rigid carrier secured with a seat belt.

Exercise: A healthy bird is an active bird. A parrot must be provided with sufficient exercise (see page 57). I believe many incidents of aggression can be averted if the bird has adequate physical exercise.

Preferred handling: The less-than-favorite person should have the opportunity to handle the bird only in desirable situations. Going to the play

area, to the shower (if the bird likes to bathe), to the TV room, and to the dinner table are excellent opportunities for the bird to be reinforced for good behavior toward a perceived enemy who is providing transportation. Many birds that are usually absolute "vampires" are sweet as can be when they are wet. It's a perfect opportunity to work on handling skills.

Less favored handling: The very favorite person has the responsibility of performing less desirable tasks with the bird—bathing the bird that hates bathing, putting a wound-up bird to bed, perhaps even grooming. Although a shy bird is best groomed professionally, I believe some Amazon and macaw owners establish dominance very well by grooming the bird at an appropriate moment.

Hormone therapy: In addition to training and aggression-prevention adjustments in the environment, hormone therapy is available from an avian veterinarian. As with any drug therapy for behavioral reasons in humans, this is probably a treatment of last resort and should be undertaken only with great care.

I have many times seen parrots switch from persecuting a person to loving that person as a result of a rescue. If a bird is picking on a particular person, that is the person who should "rescue" Paco from perceived danger. Watch for naturally occurring opportunities, such as the groomer or veterinarian. It may not work the first time or two, but if you take advantage of every opportunity, this technique can really turn a relationship around. A practicing bird behavior consultant may be able to assist you in setting up an artificial rescue scenario. This is best done only with expert supervision.

Changing loyalties: When handling a parrot to compensate for overbonding, watch for signs of changing loyalties and adjust the behavior program accordingly. A parrot may switch favorites from time to time.

It happens with people, too. For 13 years growing up in a small town, I watched my mother interact socially with a group of about 20 very parrot-like women. I got to watch their relationships evolve. One year Mom would be close with Mrs. A—best buddies, bridge partners, and confidants. The next year they were worst enemies, wouldn't play bridge at the same table, and acted like strangers when forced to come face to face in our small community.

Meanwhile Mom would be really close with Mrs. B—shopping and telephone buddies and, of course, bridge partners, until the inevitable falling out. Then Mom would have a close relationship with Mrs. C, until one day she would wake up and realize that her *real true friend* was none other than Mrs. A! Then she would cycle through the whole community again.

A parrot in the house for many years is also likely to change alliances for almost any perceived "mistreatment" by a beloved human. Sometimes a change in alliance can be traced to a single incident—an acci-

A bird being transported—even in an automobile—should be contained in a hard-sided carrier. (green-cheeked Amazon)

dent during social interaction in which the bird is frightened or injured. A period of "abandonment"—a vacation or return to work—can trigger a change in loyalties by the parrot. The changing of alliances by a parrot isn't as sophisticated as the same process in my mother's group of bridge players. While Mom's friends merely ignored and snubbed one another, a sexually mature, overbonded parrot may *actually attack almost anyone, including the one it loves.*

A bird may change loyalties for no apparent reason, but may be responding to some mysterious life cycle. I believe I have observed emotional cycles of four years in large cockatoos. I know one umbrella cockatoo who loved his Mom and tried to kill his Dad for the first four years of his life, then loved his Dad and tried to kill his Mom until he was eight. Then at the age of 11½ he was showing signs of switching again, when the owners decided they couldn't

Some of the parrots with the smallest beaks can deliver very painful bites. (green-cheeked conure)

handle him any more and set him up to breed.

Because of the configuration of the beak—with two points on the lower mandible and one point on the upper mandible—the cockatoo can administer an extremely damaging and painful bite. This particular bird was quite intimidating and actually dangerous. It had been hand-fed, but its "natural" personality was allowed full latitude, and no aggression-prevention techniques were in place. At the age of 11 this enormous, beautiful, male umbrella cockatoo did not successfully respond to the initiation of behavioral training.

Just because a young baby bird is the "sweetest little thing you ever saw," doesn't mean it won't be dangerous when it reaches sexual maturity. This umbrella cockatoo might still be a pet today if step-ups had been consistently reinforced and aggression-prevention techniques had been started sooner. As it is, he is proudly making very sweet babies, and I (almost) don't miss his affection. It is possible that his gentle disposition will return when his "breeding lifetime" is passed, and we will retrain him to be the sweet pet he was in his youth.

Occasionally we see greys and Amazons, particularly double yellow heads and yellow napes, that cannot be handled at all for many years. However, some of those very ornery parrots that have terrorized humans for a generation or more might suddenly demonstrate a desire for human handling. I have recently seen several older birds do an about-face and become handleable after years of fierceness. I have, on several occasions, introduced companion birds, believed to be mean for many years, to happy relationships with new families or new generations of their longtime family. Although it lasts much longer than the terrible two's, I believe that nippy seasonal phases eventually pass.

If your winged terror has been a monster for years, but suddenly demonstrates different behaviors such as screaming for attention or begging, it may be ready to return to the "family affection fold." In time, even the worst "vampire" may respond to a little more training and a little more love.

Chapter Five
Lifestyle Issues

Whether a companion parrot lives in a house or condo, town or country, with a large family or single person, human lifestyles and lifestyle issues can affect the bird's behavior and quality of life. The healthier the human lifestyle, the easier things should be for the bird.

The Diet*

A bird's health and disposition can suffer if dietary balance is off in any "direction." Too much of anything— even fruits or vegetables—can have health consequences over the long term. That's important because so many parrots have the potential to live so many years.

Obesity is not uncommon in birds that do not fly or at least flap vigorously every day. Overeating or selectively overeating certain elements in the diet can lead to obesity. Because of its high oil content, seed is a common culprit here. A careful, meticulous person may be able to get by with feeding seed instead of pellets as long as the seed is fresh, but seed is probably best offered sprouted, and sprouts have to be fresh.

The easiest way to provide appropriate nutrition for a companion parrot is to trust the professionals and feed a scientifically-formulated pellet-based diet supplemented with healthy table food, mostly vegetables and fruits. Sweet potatoes, squash, pumpkin, beets, broccoli, carrots, peas, green beans, radishes, mangoes, papaya, melons, peppers, leaf lettuce, and tomatoes can add essential nutrients, as well as color and variety. Other healthy table food includes small amounts of lean meat, pasta, rice, beans, whole grain bread, and eggs. Dairy products such as yogurt and cheese can supply extra calcium, but birds don't digest dairy products easily, so they should be given only occasionally in small amounts.

---

*With Dianalee Deter, correspondence and conversations

A companion parrot and its environment must be protected from one another. (scarlet macaw)

Avoid avocado and chocolate, which can be toxic. Foods high in fat, salt, caffeine, sugar, artificial flavors, and artificial colors should be avoided. As with humans, companion parrots can become both fat and malnourished if they consume mass quantities of potato chips, French fries, ice cream, soda pop, candy, cake, cookies, and other junk foods.

Feeding schedule, style, or strategy can be nearly as important as what is fed. If large quantities of food are constantly available, the bird will naturally choose to eat as much as it wants of whatever it prefers. I believe parrots are best fed only as much as they can completely consume in 30–40 minutes. Parrots fed twice daily in this manner probably eat a better balance, waste less food, and easily take treats used for training during windows of opportunity when food isn't available.

An occasional complication in a new home is discontinuance of independent eating. Weighing the bird every day at the same time, preferably before it eats in the morning, safeguards against problems related to failure to eat as well as other health issues. Small weight fluctuations of 5 or 10 grams are not dangerous, but if the bird loses more than 10–20 percent of what it weighed when it came home, it may be in trouble.

Ask your veterinarian about your bird's ideal weight. When implementing schedule feeding or other diet changes, be sure the bird does not quit eating, especially if it's a small parrot. With schedule feeding, the bird's weight will likely normalize, with fat or pudgy birds losing weight and thin birds often gaining. In addition, schedule-fed birds are less likely to be fussy eaters or to waste or throw food.

Companion parrots that don't fly—whether it's their choice or yours—have fewer opportunities for exercise. Consumption of too many calories can easily result in too much energy and not enough ways to use that energy, which can contribute to nippiness, feather-destructive behavior, or excessive screaming. Poorly-nourished parrots might also be non-vocal or inactive.

A bird unaccustomed to eating a variety of food might not realize that fruits and vegetables are actually edible. Having another bird as a role model is extremely helpful. Human role models are helpful, too. Parrots often beg (flatten themselves, lean toward the food, and quiver) or try to steal whatever people around them are eating. This is natural, since eating is a "flock" behavior. Encouraging this behavior makes introducing new foods easier and helps the bird feel like part of the family. A companion parrot may, within reason, eat healthy human food, but don't forget that one piece of pizza, one inch square, might contain more salt, oil, and calories than the bird should eat in a whole day. Huge, human-sized treats of anything, whether it's pizza or popcorn, can destroy the nutritional balance of a good parrot diet.

Ask your veterinarian about your bird's ideal weight. (blue-crowned mealy Amazon)

On the Shoulder

The practice of allowing a medium or large hookbill access to the shoulder upon demand is vehemently and adamantly discouraged by many long-time aviculturists and parrot behavior professionals. This is not because the parrot allowed regularly on the shoulder is "usually" dangerous or even "frequently" dangerous, but because of the very severe nature of potential injuries. It's fun to snuggle with Paco on my shoulder, but is it worth losing an eye? There remains the very real threat of permanent damage to the face and to personal effectiveness and self-esteem.

Displaced Aggression

An initial incident of displaced aggression against a primary human typically goes something like this:

Although Mary Lou had lived with budgies and cockatiels for years, Paco was her first large hookbill. At the age of ten, this formerly hand-fed blue-fronted Amazon had been accompanying Mary Lou on outings to public schools, malls, and other educational events for eight years. While they had some behavior counseling through the developmental period, Mary Lou did not think it necessary to banish the baby from the shoulder, require him to respond dependably to the *step-up* command, or house him below eye level.

Mary Lou lived alone but dated Terry, who took a hands-off approach with Paco because of past incidents of aggression. Mary Lou always found it rather amusing to see her 350-gram bird abuse her 180-pound boyfriend, who occasionally teased the bird.

Mary Lou took Paco, with wing feathers always meticulously trimmed, to and from the car on her shoulder. Carrying a portable perch and a bag of food treats and toys, she was walking out the door one morning when Terry leaned over to plant a good-bye kiss on her left cheek. Paco—on the right shoulder—screamed, fanned his tail, pinpointed his eyes, and in a blink ripped Mary Lou's right cheek open. The wound tore straight down from the outside corner of her eye, requiring stitches. Miraculously, the eye was unscathed.

With the smaller domesticated parrots—budgies, cockatiels, and lovebirds—danger is minimal. Owners of Amazons are at great risk of severe injury, as are owners of macaws, African greys, and cockatoos, and to a lesser extent caiques, conures, and lories. I believe a noisy, nippy "shoulder bird" conure is a creature very often relegated to a back room for the rest of its life—a life which may be prematurely short as a result of neglect abuse.

Like puppies, human-bonded, hand-fed baby parrots are awesomely sweet. Their "sweet, sweet baby" period may last much longer than a dog's; but just as with dogs, without prevention training, aggression is just down the road. A "shoulder bird" will begin expressing overt aggression against people and animals approaching its "shoulder human." This behavior is usually easy to correct during the developmental period when the jealousy is expressed to defend territory and define status. If this behavior is allowed to persist, the "shoulder bird" will eventually express displaced aggression against the "shoulder human" because it is so enraged by jealousy, which includes issues of status, protection, and sexuality.

Both overt aggression and displaced aggression escalate with maturity. If aggression by the bird against everyone but you is tolerated, there is a real possibility that someday that bird will express displaced aggression against you. Displaced aggression toward the primary person is often more violent than any previous incident of overt aggression toward others.

The injury in an initial incident of displaced aggression against the favorite person is not always so severe but may be worse and may be permanently disfiguring. Injuries include, but are not limited to, damaged ear, eye, ripped-open lips that do not recover full movement, or broken nose, finger, or arm.

In my opinion, there is no such thing as a "safe" shoulder. There are, however, ways to minimize the danger. For example, there is a recognizable phenomenon that many parrots who are absolute bullies in their own territory are quite nice as pie in public. This accounts for the many beautiful macaws providing photo opportunities for tourists in markets and beaches around the world. (These birds are usually perched at chest level or below, which inhibits the development of height-related aggression.)

A "safer" shoulder, therefore, is in a location about which the well-trained parrot is not territorial and is not in the presence of another bird, person, or object of whom the bird is jealous.

This away-from-home/good behavior phenomenon is sometimes used to defend the reputation of a parrot who is charged with being "vicious" in its own territory. A friend of a friend who had an absolutely charming blue-and-gold macaw lived in a small apartment building. In that building on the same floor level lived a man with a cat. There were no screens on the windows, and if the man with the cat left his window open and the man with the macaw left his window open, the cat would go in and harass the macaw. Of course, there was much animosity, because neither man could close his windows without the apartment's becoming uncomfortably hot. One day, the macaw owner returned to his almost all-white apartment to find it reduced to a bloody mess. Examination of the macaw cage revealed part of a cat's foot in the bottom of the cage.

I do not believe the cat survived, and the macaw owner was charged with keeping a vicious animal in the city. The macaw owner sued the cat owner for property damage, and everybody went to court. Now the blue-and-gold macaw can be very intimidating to the uninitiated, and although it has the most dependable disposition of the common companion macaws, a blue-and-gold in a cage can defend its territory quite aggressively.

This bird was a perfect angel in court. He went readily and sweetly to anyone and was exonerated of his "self-defense" crime. He might not have fared so well if an Animal Control Officer in a uniform who knew little about parrot behavior had evaluated his disposition in his own territory, especially in the presence of a person, bird, animal, or object of which the bird was jealous.

Of course, a parrot with a poorly reinforced step-up response should *not* be allowed on the shoulder. A parrot that will refuse to step up and that runs around to the other shoulder or to the middle of the back is demonstrating a controlling behavior usually consistent with a bird that will bite.

A "shoulder human" can be the object of displaced aggression against the telephone. How dare Mom/Dad spend so much time with that thing on the shoulder? A safer "shoulder human" will put the bird down before picking up the phone.

As the parrot reaches sexual maturity, we will see an increase in hormonally induced hostility. Because these periods of hormone activity are probably stimulated by photo periods (the length of daylight hours), they will often occur on approximately the same date every year. If you are the victim of a nasty hormonal rage, mark the date on your calendar and transfer it to your new calendar next year. Discontinue any shoulder time and be especially watchful for aggressive behavior beginning a week or two before the documented date of last year's aggressive behavior.

It is a good practice to wear eyeglasses when allowing the bird on the shoulder, particularly during the time of anticipated increased aggression. If the bird is stimulated to express overt or displaced aggression toward the face, it may bite the glasses instead of flesh.

Effective long-term behavioral groundwork, including well-established dominant status over the bird, will allow you some "safer shoulder" time through the bird's first ten years. Many—probably most—macaws, Amazons, and African greys over the age of ten years should not be allowed *any* shoulder time. I repeat: real danger may be infrequent, but the risks are *very great!*

Parrots and Children

Many children have allergies or live in a setting where cats or dogs are unwelcome. If the rest of the family has a tolerance for noise (bird song), feathers, and a little mess, then birds can find a happy niche in their family "flock."

It is well documented that people talk more to their birds than to any other type of companion animal. While owners of companion birds don't always experience the physical closeness we feel with a dog or cat who might share our bed, I believe we are intellectually closer to our avian companions than we are to their less communicative mammalian cousins. Because of this close verbal and intellectual interaction, I believe parrots are excellent companion animals for children, particularly for an only child.

Depending upon the temperament and disposition of the child, one might choose to begin with the inexpensive and readily available American parakeet, or budgie. Although these colorful little creatures are every bit as smart as many other parrots, and more charming and beautiful, they are fragile and not particularly long-lived. I see many would-be juvenile aviculture careers cut short by the untimely, accidental death of one of these sweet, lovely creatures. It can be an emotionally devastating, guilt-inducing experience for a sensitive child, who might then avoid birds for life.

Lovebirds and cockatiels are great for careful children, but I prefer to see youngsters, particularly rambunctious ones, with a sturdier bird. My favorite bird for children is the Quaker parakeet. These little companions are easily bred and relatively inexpensive in the areas where they are available. They are noisy but seldom aggressive.

For the bird's safety, a companion bird acquired for a child must be considered a family responsibility. It's a good idea to provide lots of behavior training and backup care for the first bird. It is also wise to have a standing appointment with a groomer so that the bird never has the opportunity to grow enough wing feather for flight. In addition to fly-aways, common and predictable dangers for children's birds are drowning in a glass or the

toilet, being slammed in a door, being closed in drawers, being sat on, stepped on, or rolled on.

Sharing life with a bird provides children with opportunities to develop a sense of responsibility, decision-making abilities, and leadership potential. With a reasonably sturdy bird and a little planning, the benefits outweigh the risks. I have seen many youthful bird lovers grow into fine, responsible young adults.

A companion parrot and young children must be carefully supervised and protected from one another. (yellow-naped Amazon)

Parrots and Other Pets

Because birds are social by nature, and because they relate to their group of companions—regardless of shape—it is not unusual for parrots to have lasting meaningful relationships with other pets. Although the predatory nature of some carnivorous pets can be hazardous to birds, sensitive introductions and pet "family planning" can ensure animal harmony in the home. Supervision of the new relationship as well as a carefully timed squirt or bop on the too-interested nose will guide an established, well-adjusted dog or cat to happy acceptance of a new bird in the home. Watch out for provocative behavior and establish limits the animals can understand.

People are often surprised to learn that I have both cats and birds. Indeed, one of the questions most frequently asked of a bird behavior consultant is, "Is it okay to have a cat with a bird?"

The answer depends upon the bird(s) and the cat(s). A macaw or other large parrot can easily handle almost any domestic feline, but a small finch or budgie may be lost to even a slightly predatory cat. Actually, bird-initiated aggression toward the other pets is at least as problematic as aggression from the other pets.

Aviculturists possessing large collections of birds frequently have stores of foodstuffs and grains that are attractive to rodents. A cat is a logical addition to such an environment and performs well as natural rodent control. A cat introduced to companion birds as a young kitten usually becomes completely trustworthy with *the kind of birds it was raised with*. Also, it is not necessary to starve a cat to induce it to catch mice. I suspect that kitties that don't go after birds may demonstrate increased enthusiasm for hunting mice.

A cat is a welcome diversion for alleviating boredom for a companion parrot that spends the day alone. Avian and feline pets form warm, playful, and sometimes romantic relationships. My cockatiel, Pearl, is often observed "soliciting" (with sexual postures) either her bell or her favorite kitty.

Adoring birds sometimes groom cat whiskers and fur, but I believe the most common bird-initiated cat play is "Come to me, come to me, go away." In this game the bird calls the cat (many birds literally use "here, kitty, kitty"), displays for the cat, hangs upside down to attract the cat, then bites, bops, or threatens kitty when it comes near.

My kitties like to steal toys dropped by Kaku, the cockatoo, whose favorite pastime is unhooking her numerous toys and dropping them to attract the kitties. Once the kitties are stationed under the cage investigating what toys have recently been dropped there, they are then "bombed" with other toys from above.

Cats are attracted to the smell and movements of birds. Smaller birds are more enticing because of their fluttering. When adding a bird to a home with cats, parrots—particularly larger ones—have the advantage. They are less attractive because they flap their wings with more decisive, less frenetic actions. Their hard beaks, intimidating size, domineering personalities, and naturally loud voices provide all the built-in socialization needed to protect from and usually dominate or befriend any domestic feline.

If it appears that a kitty is "stalking" the bird, a couple of squirts of water directed at the kitty's face can terminate the kitty's interest immediately. A kitten squirted for inappropriate attention only a few times will usually discontinue "stalking" interest in a pet bird. With very little encouragement well-fed kitties usually forget their instincts to hunt birds. Although many cats can be trusted with even the smallest finches, canaries, budgies, lovebirds, and cockatiels, it is unwise to introduce smaller, soft-billed birds into homes with adult cats that have not been previously socialized to accept that kind of bird.

Keepers of small birds may acquire a very young kitten, training it to respect pet birds from that first awesome day in the new home. It is helpful for a large bird to "demonstrate" the need for respect with a supervised nip on kitten nose, ear, or tail; but usually a squirt or two of water carefully timed when feline attention is on the bird will convince the kitty that those feathers are off limits.

When adding a cat to an established "bird home," a trial visit by a "bird-socialized" kitty will demonstrate whether the bird likes cats. Although most pet birds are delighted and naturally curious, very rarely, a bird that has been previously traumatized by a cat may be emotionally unable to cope with one. Probably the smallest bird that can be successfully introduced into a home with a slightly predatory adult cat is a lovebird. These tiny pugnacious parrots can sometimes get the best of even a seasoned hunter. An acquaintance of mine says that in spite of great care on her part, the neighbor's Siamese cat gained access to her home and stalked her peach-faced lovebird playing in the kitchen sink. Hearing the sound of crashing pots, she found the poor cat streaking around the kitchen with an angry lovebird fiercely clenching his tail.

The smallest bird that can be successfully introduced into a home with a predatory cat probably is the quaker (about 5 ounces or 140–150 g). Noisy and somewhat nippy in multiples, these charming little clowns are excellent single birds who usually have no trouble dominating a mere domestic feline.

Years ago, I reluctantly recommended a Quaker to a friend with two very predatory cats. She was determined to rescue a plucked, stressed-out, bare-bellied Quaker. Imagine my surprise when I visited a few months later and found a fully-feathered parrot playing with the "hunters" and eating dry cat food out of their bowl on the floor!

Kitties who play with avian buddies should have their claws clipped regularly to prevent accidental (or on purpose) scratches. Even if the bird looks all right and acts all right, any bird whose skin has been scraped or punctured by a cat requires immediate antibiotic therapy from an avian veterinarian to prevent the development of pasteurella, a fatal bacterial infection.

While I find bird-socialized domestic felines to be excellent parrot companions, I do not believe a ferret can be trusted with *any* bird. They do not seem to be capable of changing their extremely predatory instincts against birds. I often hear of ferrets killing even large Psittaciformes such as cockatoos and macaws. Cockatiels, budgies, and lories haven't a chance.

Although dogs can be very dangerous to parrots, dogs and parrots also can form warm, devoted relationships. However, an unfamiliar dog probably represents a greater danger to medium and larger hook-bills than a cat. Because of the extreme differences between the many types and sizes of dogs, it is much harder to generalize about their behavior toward companion parrots. I have taken histories of dogs killing birds in instances of predatory aggression, overt aggression against the bird, and displaced aggression toward the bird in response to anger against some other person or situation.

Some of the "mouthier" types of parrots may be incompatible with barking or noisy dogs. Many parrots are at particular risk for developing abnormal screaming in response to barking dogs.

Introducing a dog into a bird home is thoughtfully preceded by a trial visit by a "bird-socialized" dog to determine whether the bird likes dogs. A bird that has been traumatized by a dog may be unable to tolerate one. I see many more parrots that fear dogs than parrots that fear cats. It is much easier to socialize young animals, although a well-adjusted older dog may accept a new bird immediately and without question. Because of the enormous variety of dog dispositions and temperaments, I believe the introduction of a dog into a home with a parrot should be made with the guidance of a dog behavior professional.

Reptiles usually represent minimal danger, although large snakes kept at liberty in the home can prey on pet birds. Pond and aquarium fish are not considered a threat to birds, although their aquatic environments

Stealing food from other pets is dangerous and unhealthy for parrots. (African grey parrot)

are attractive and present a drowning hazard.

Although interspecies dangers exist and multiple-pet interactions should be well supervised, it is not unusual for companion pets to save each other's lives. Dogs have often alerted owners to dangers to pet birds just as birds often alert other pets and humans to dangers.

The Bird Who Spends the Day Alone

One of the ironic elements of companion parrot ownership is that often when persons can finally *afford* that special large hookbill, they have to go to work all day in order to pay for it. Just as dogs left alone all day develop behavior problems, parrots left alone all day will, at the very least, be extremely demanding of attention in the evening. They may express anger through aggression, they may scream incessantly (or maybe just when you're on the telephone), they may begin chewing their feathers off, or destroying anything they can get their beaks on.

Just as children left alone all day can be expected to get into trouble, birds left alone all day can get into some surprising predicaments.

A bird that is left alone all day appreciates any companionship activities available. Breakfast is a traditionally shared meal. Morning grooming activities—bathing, show-

A parrot left alone all day may develop attention-demanding behaviors. (yellow-naped Amazon)

ering or shaving, combing or blowing the hair dry—are excellent side-by-side activities to share with your parrot(s). If you have access to a telephone at work and a telephone machine at home, it's not a bad idea to call your bird to say "Hi!" or whatever other words you are hoping the bird will incorporate into its vocabulary. This serves the dual purpose of providing a little diversion during the day and a little reinforcement for speech training.

A parrot is at particular risk for development of territorial aggression if it stays home all the time. It is highly desirable to take the bird on outings, perhaps to short work days, weekends in the country, or even simply to the shopping mall. Excursions, particularly with the less-than-favorite person, can help to ensure that the bird will not be phobic in new situations or with other people.

Bird Versus Machine

One of my clients, an owner of two cockatoos, vacuumed her bird room every morning for several years with the same upright vacuum cleaner. Every day she left the vacuum cleaner in the same place in the sunroom where the birds lived at liberty. One day (maybe about the 700th day the vacuum cleaner had been sitting in that room) on her return from work she found that the birds had completely destroyed the vacuum cleaner. Apparently the vacuum cleaner parts were mostly plastic, and she affirmed that there was no piece left larger than 2 to 4 inches (5–10 cm) in diameter. The cockatoos had never touched the vacuum cleaner before.

Just as it's a good idea to take your bird from window to window to show the bird the glass it might fly into, or from room to room while acclimating the bird to a new home, excursions to work will increase the bird's understanding of your behavior. An excursion to work will "demonstrate" to the bird that you have important "foraging" to do away from the "nest site."

If possible to accomplish safely, you may also choose to leave the bird alone in the work environment for a short time, maybe on a Saturday, so that it can see how boring that work environment really is. In a rare application of the "lesser of evils" training technique, the bird left briefly on a too-small-to-be-entertaining perch in a deserted office will see that there's something worse than being left alone in the stimulating, familiar home environment.

Another pet can also provide daytime diversions in the absence of human companionship. I think the easiest adjunct for this "ecological balancing" role is either a cat or an aquarium within the bird's sight. An additional bird can easily cause jealousy, overt and displaced aggression, screaming, or several other negative behaviors as an expression of sibling rivalry by a bonded-to-a-human pet. Although dogs are excellent potential avian companions, they have many specialized environmental and training needs that make them more difficult to incorporate into the household.

A healthy parrot that has started the morning with bathing and grooming activity will spend a good amount of energy on that chore and will nap midday. Then, before Mom/Dad gets home, the bird can be awakened by a television on a timer.

Birds have excellent hearing and appreciate music, but eyesight is their most acutely developed sense. Although the audio companionship of a radio is beneficial, I believe a bird given both sight and sound stimulation will be less demanding as a result of having more of its sensory needs met. Television is the easiest way to provide this stimulation in the owner's absence. Someday someone will produce a visually stimulating videotape especially for this purpose. There is such a tape now available for cats, and it actually works pretty well for birds. It has lots of chattering birds and squirrels. My own bird, Portia, an Amazon, loves the video for cats as well as cartoons, *Jeopardy*, *Family Feud*, Tarzan movies, football games, and the "William Tell" and "Thieving Magpie" overtures.

If you don't have a timer, leave the radio on all day. It provides some stimulation and is less intrusive than all-day TV. For larger, more intelligent hookbills, however, I believe the television on a timer is better. Paco will not have adequate opportunity for rest if you leave the television on all the time you are gone, but if you set the TV to come on a couple of hours before you get home, the bird will have a little time for independent action, will have used up a little energy, and will be ready to see you, but not demand all your time and all your energy all evening.

That is not to say that you can ignore the bird. Just as a cat that expects attention will "trip" the owner until it receives its expected daily allotment of attention, a bird will communicate its attention needs in unmistakable ways—talking, screaming, banging things around.

To avert the development of problematic screaming, immediately upon return from work give the bird some face-to-face attention. Let the bird out of the cage, talk to it, and do a little aerobic exercise. Give the bird a favorite toy that has been withheld during the day and go on about your business, preferably allowing the bird to be in the room with you. If the bird has learned to entertain itself and has not been overnurtured, it will be quite content with side-by-side activities for most of the rest of the evening.

Hazards in the Home

Wings and the ability to fly appear to be the most common component contributing to indoor bird deaths. Whether the death is caused by a ceiling fan, a toilet, or a frying pan, the means by which the cause of death was achieved is usually by flying into trouble. But even birds with trimmed wing feathers can often find surprising hazards in places we might never imagine.

Water is probably the most common cause of death, as a bird that cannot breathe dies within seconds. Drowning can happen very quickly in extremely unlikely ways: head down in a half full glass on the table, floating in an unattended hot tub, sink, or aquarium.

Because of their active and curious natures, parrots are vulnerable to being closed into closets and drawers. Behind drowning accidents, being squashed or suffocated is probably the second most common cause of death in the companion parrot. Many of these little characters do really like to cuddle, and it is not unusual for a bird to snuggle under an Afghan or quilt that might be subsequently sat on with great force. Being squashed or suffocated is an

Fire!

One of my clients, a student, shared a house near a university campus with several other students. The bird owner was well aware that Teflon fumes were poisonous to birds under certain circumstances, but had little control over the cookware used by his housemates. One night a roommate came home from an evening of beer drinking and decided to make spaghetti. After placing a pot of water on the stove, he fell asleep. Two hours later, the owner was awakened by the parrot calling out his name. Rushing downstairs, he found the Teflon coating on the pot in flames and was able to extinguish the fire. Although the bird saved the lives of humans and other pets, in this situation the bird did not survive.

especially common fate among smaller parrots that are allowed to sleep with humans.

Another of the greatest threats to indoor birds, because they so frequently flee danger, is the danger from other pets. These birds may be large enough to handle most cats, but they are just tempting enough to be an attractive chase for a dog. Especially, a gregarious, exploratory bird in an unfamiliar environment who does not fear dogs must be protected from seeking them out, for many birds, even small ones, are known to provoke dogs. A dog that is repeatedly provoked can hardly be punished for fighting back even though the offensive Brotegeris or Quaker may be only a mouthful to the dog.

Parrots can also fall victim to playing accidents. Many are exceptional acrobats who love to dive and spin and swing. They think they are circus performers, but they work without a net, and they occasionally miss their objective. A broken neck during active play is a rare but occasionally reported cause of death of companion parrots, especially Poicephalus and lories. This is one of the compelling reasons for the use of branches with bark rather than smooth hardwood dowel perches.

Other types of playing accidents are also often reported. Parrots love to stick their heads into things: loops of string, too-large cage bars, and other unusual spaces. Sometimes if the perch is too close to the food or water bowl, a bird might improvise a way to get its head stuck. Amazons, cockatoos, and macaws are famous for hanging themselves. Be sure that any loops are eliminated from string, fabric, or leather toys. Rigid rings should be large enough that the bird's whole body can pass through. Replace all small clips, split rings, and small quick links with large gauge quick links at least 1½ inch long (see section on toys).

Parrots also love to play with what humans play with, so they are usually very interested in whatever is in the ash tray. Not only can a curious bird be burned by cigarettes, but also, it can be poisoned by nicotine.

Roaming, unsupervised companion parrots are vulnerable to various types of chewing accidents. While they have no saliva and electrocution is rare, these birds can be electrocuted if they chew in just the wrong place at the wrong time. Especially, roaming on the floor can lead to illness related to unseen microorganisms or unsanitary conditions on the floor.

Exposure to toxins such as lead and zinc, especially by ingestion, can be fatal. Common toxins in the home include aerosols, pesticides, insecticides, medications, avocado, chocolate, alcohol, coffee, some incense, strongly scented candles, room deodorants, diffenbachia, philodendron, and some other poisonous house plants. Moldy foods are also potentially dangerous.

Several types of kitchen fumes, including those generated by oven cleaners are problematic. Be sure to remove a bird from the kitchen and adjoining rooms, preferably remove them from the home when cleaning the oven. If oven cleaners are used, non-aerosol ones are least likely to harm birds. Be sure to provide adequate ventilation, fans, and open windows to prevent the accumulation of gaseous toxins related to oven cleaning.

Misuse of polymer coated and impregnated cookware such as Polytetrafluorethelyene, also known as Teflon, can kill all birds in the home virtually immediately. Fumes from other polymer impregnated products, such as pans, coffee makers, irons, and ironing board covers, can also kill a parrot if the product is heated over 530°F (280°C). Even though

Michael the Parakeet

Callie Rennison wrote an article for *Bird Talk* a few years back describing a harrowing experience involving a variety of birds belonging to her family. On the day before Thanksgiving, in 1997, as her parents prepared to leave for work, they heard an unusual thing. Michael, the parakeet, who usually rang his bell only in the evenings was vigorously ringing his bell.

When her mom investigated the persistent ringing, she found the bird room in flames. Quickly removing the birds from the room, Callie's parents found that their own panic made very simple tasks difficult. Two budgies, including Michael, were lost in the fire, but the parrots and two humans survived because of the warning provided by the parakeet.*

*Rennison, *Bird Talk* (September 1998): pages 72–79.

most self-cleaning ovens are known to contain no polymer coatings, a coated oven rack, skillet, or drip pan left in during cleaning can emit fumes that can kill the birds in minutes.

I have often counseled in homes in which owners were well aware of the danger and owned only one piece of polymer coated cookware. Not infrequently, however, this is the exact pan chosen by guests (who are unaware of the danger to the bird) in the home. Many of the polymer fume deaths I have documented have involved a person other than the owner and inattention related to alcohol use. The story usually goes something like this: a roommate or guest in the home comes home late after enjoying a few drinks, decides to fix tea or spaghetti, sits down, and falls asleep leaving the coated pan to burn. The pan catches on fire; the birds scream to warn the humans just before they die.

Inattention caused by alcohol use can lead to a huge variety of bird accidents in the home. If you have been drinking, leave the cookware in the cabinet and the bird in the cage. If a polymer pan is burned, and the bird is still breathing (rare), get it immediately into fresh air and rush it to the veterinarian before its respiratory system closes down. Something can be done if it is done quickly. Because accidents can happen in the best-meaning homes, just throw all polymer coated or impregnated cookware away. It is not worth the risk of losing a treasured bird because somebody burned a pan.

In Case of Emergency: Disaster Preparations

Many companion parrots live a very long time. That means that statistically, if there is one disaster in a typical geographic area every twenty-five years, every parrot larger than a cockatiel may well be involved in some kind of disaster during its lifetime. Whether threatened by a major natural disaster, such as a hurricane, tornado, blizzard, or earthquake, or a simple burned skillet, caged birds are completely dependent on humans to rescue them.

Early Warning System

Whether it is a natural disaster or a household fire, the birds' behavior is often the first clue that something out-of-the-ordinary is going on. It is not unusual for a bird to lose its life warning humans of fire, even kitchen fires or other localized fires. This can be the best argument for bird homes to be bountifully populated with smoke detectors. And, of course, smoke detectors are only as dependable as the batteries inside, so they must be checked regularly to see that they are operating. Safety experts recommend establishing two regular days a year to check the smoke detectors. Some people say check them on Labor Day and Memorial Day; I usually check mine at Christmas and the Fourth of July.

Evacuation

No matter what actual process is causing an avian emergency, the first and foremost component of danger to indoor birds is toxic fumes. Fumes resulting from even an insignificant-seeming event can kill the birds in the house before they affect anyone or anything else. Fires, even small fires, can kill a bird whose sensitive respiratory system can succumb in minutes to all manner of toxic fumes. If you suspect that any synthetic fiber or plastic has been heated sufficiently to release fumes—whether it is polytetrafluoroethylene (sometimes called Teflon), plastic mini blinds, plastic bottles, carpeting, or chemicals—remove all birds from the home immediately.

It is important to have an appropriate carrier ready to take the bird from the home. That means, provide a carrier that had the paper changed after its last use, and provide one adequately sized carrier for each bird or other animal. If there is only one dirty carrier and half a dozen various sized birds and a puppy, some of the birds might wind up being released from a high rise fire or other situation where options are limited. It is better than nothing. You can probably catch them later.

Do not expect to be able to evacuate a bird usually housed on the second floor in a carrier kept in the back of a closet in the basement. Carriers must be situated adjacent to the area where the bird is kept.

It is a good idea to test equipment and proposed evacuation procedures by doing them. Practicing will enable humans to know how long the evacuation procedures take and maximize efficiency in performing the evacuation. Practicing will also show the birds what is expected of them and enable them to more easily cooperate when the chips are down.

Fire Extinguishers

While fire extinguishers might help to save the structure, birds succumb so quickly to fumes, the best proce-

dure begins with evacuating the birds. Even professional firefighters will probably chose to remove all humans and animals before proceeding to fight the fire. It is helpful, of course, to have some way of advising rescue personnel about the number of animals and the type of evacuation procedures expected. There are recognizable stickers available to put on entrances to advise numbers and locations of animals. Additional stickers should advise where to find carriers, and in the case of high rises, ropes should be easily accessible for lowering carriers.

"Typical" Emergencies

In case of a blizzard, a snow storm, or just an interruption of power during cold weather, do not become overly concerned with immediately generating heat. Most alternative heat sources, such as propane or kerosene stoves, generate fumes, and birds are much more sensitive to fumes than they are to cold. A healthy bird with a covered cage should be able to tolerate at least a day or two of subfreezing temperature, presuming it is protected from moisture and drafts that would threaten to freeze its feet. Feed occasional warm foods to the birds, if possible. If there is electricity, but no heat, as in a gas failure, you can provide a small amount of heat for a bird cage with an electric light bulb situated close to the cage.

Fumes from damaged gas lines will be a danger after tornadoes and earthquakes, but during disasters that threaten buildings, seek shelter from falling walls and flying debris. Take the birds, in rigid carriers, with you into the bathtub and cover your heads with a mattress (be sure to leave a way for oxygen to get in).

Hurricanes represent a special danger because hurricanes occur in temperate regions where aviaries may be situated outdoors. Of course these birds must be moved indoors when a storm is approaching. Lack of planned evacuation procedures could prove disastrous for many birds, especially in large breeding facilities.

If you are actually leaving the area, such as for a flood or hurricane or suspect that water supplies may be contaminated or interrupted, store a two week supply of fresh water. Of course, it is a good idea to always keep at least a two week extra supply of basic diet in the freezer so that if a disaster comes just as the bird's food is depleted, the bird does not wind up living on Cheerios for a fortnight. Although, in a pinch, you know, Cheerios or other unsweetened human cereal can keep a stranded companion bird alive for a few days or even a few weeks.

Recapture: When Your Parrot Flies Away

Accidental escape is one of the most common calamities suffered by companion parrots. In the past, escaped parrots were considered potential agricultural pests because wild-caught birds could survive easily in the wild. However, an escaped hand-fed parrot's chances of long-term survival are not particularly good, especially in areas where food or water is scarce or where there is raptor activity or extended periods of very cold (below freezing) weather.

Fortunately, today's hand-fed parrots know where "their bread is buttered." In my twenty-odd years of experience recapturing parrots in urban settings, I see that hand-fed parrots usually find accommodating humans to take care of them, usually within the first 24 hours of escape. For this reason, I expect a hand-fed parrot recapture to be primarily a public relations project.

When You Don't Know Where the Bird Is

If you don't know where the bird is, you must advertise to find it. This is a simple "numbers game." When more people hear that your bird is missing, it is more likely that the person who has your bird will be able to find you. Typically, the bird is returned by humans who have been caring for it as soon as they see advertising for the lost bird.

Call local newspapers, humane societies, animal control, local bird dealers, avian veterinarians, groomers, and recapture services. Be sure to report this lost "property" to the police. If the bird is found and the people holding the bird won't relinquish it, the police may intervene.

You must be able to prove ownership, possibly with a recorded band number, registered DNA configuration, microchipping, photos, or by records of unique physical or behavioral properties in the bird.

Place ads in the local newspapers and on church and grocery store bulletin boards. Make a flyer with a photo or a reasonable likeness of the bird. Prepare an 8½ by 11 inch (22 × 29 cm) white original so that it can be easily copied on to brightly colored paper. The flyer should contain a contact phone number; an alternate contact number, such as a pager; and the street corner or local landmark nearest to where the bird flew away. The flyer should mention small rewards available for information leading to the location of the bird and a more sizable reward for the bird's return. It is a good idea to minimize the value of the bird, possibly mentioning that the bird is not in good health, noisy, or of less-than-perfect disposition. Identifying characteristics may be mentioned, such as missing toe or banding on a particular leg. If the bird has a band, don't reveal the band number, so that the information can be used to differentiate between a person who really has your bird and an unscrupulous person who might be pretending to have your bird.

Most people will be honest and helpful. Talk with everyone you see, and make lots of flyers to post around the neighborhood and to hand to people. Use a different bright color each time the flyer is reprinted. If the recapture process lasts a while, the signs may have to be occasionally reposted after bad weather, and a new color will help people to understand that the search is still "fresh," and they should call if they see the bird. Don't forget to take your flyers down immediately upon recovering the bird. It is only polite, and in some places you may be fined if you do not take them down.

Do not give up. Keep looking. A bird doesn't usually just disappear. Somebody has it, somebody has seen it, or somebody will see it eventually. A friend told me that he lost a pair of Quakers in northern Colorado on the Fourth of July in the 1980s. Exactly one year later, also on the Fourth of July, he was contacted by a neighbor who reported that he had captured the birds in his hen house. There had been no reported sightings of the birds in this rural setting for that entire year.

When You Know Where the Bird Is

In the case of a true "recapture," when we know where the bird is, a well-bonded, hand-fed parrot will usually come willingly to the beloved owner. Expect a really good flyer to fly down. Expect a poor flyer to climb down. It is easier to lure a parrot down with jealousy than with food. Have the bird's very favorite person stand hugging the most hated person or bird or giving the bird's very favorite food to the most hated person. If you are using a live companion bird as a lure, be sure to leave it

Marty's Choice

Years before, he had been the "tax man" in my life. We met when he audited my income taxes. Years later, becoming my friend and client, Marty was vital, active, and wheelchair bound. He was the long time owner of an African grey parrot.

One summer morning, as he emerged from the shower, Marty discovered that his wife had left the back door wide open when she went to work. On that particular morning, Marty had taken Ben, the grey parrot, into the shower with him. Turning the corner to the kitchen with Ben perched on his lap, they both saw the open back door, and at that exact moment, the door behind them blew shut with a loud "Bang!"

Startled, Ben (who was scheduled for a wing trim that very day) flew out the back door. Marty, wet, dripping, and "dressed" only in a towel draped over his lap, followed out onto the patio in his rolling chair. There was Ben, perched in the fork of a young crabapple tree beside the picnic table. He was only inches out of reach, clicking and pinpointing his eyes, obviously enjoying his sunny freedom.

Marty took no time making his decision. Hoping that his neighbors were not watching, he chose his bird over modesty. Pulling himself almost upright, Marty flipped the towel over his errant grey friend, pulled him from the fork of the tree, and wheeled, naked, back to the house with an angry grey parrot wrapped in the towel.

Ben would be on time for his wing-trimming appointment, and Marty would be avoiding his neighbors for a few days.

---

protected in a cage so that it will not be endangered by predators.

Usually, if the very favorite person can reach the bird, the bird will step up onto that person's hand. That means, sometimes ladders and sometimes more elaborate climbing equipment. Use a fiberglass or wooden ladder, which reduces the possibility of electrocution, the most common cause of death in pet bird recapture.

When climbing to retrieve a bird, be sure to put a pillow case in your hip pocket so that you will not have to climb down with an angry, resistive creature. Just put the bird in the pillow case, tie a knot in it so that the bird cannot get out and then, if necessary, the pillow case can be dropped to someone on the ground. Be sure to take a favorite food to entice the bird closer, and be sure to get a good grip on the bird's foot, preferably, both feet, as you may have only one chance to do so. Do not worry about being bitten—a parrot cannot usually do much damage. Just be brave, grit your teeth, hold on, and get that bird into the pillow case.

A device called a "cherry picker" is probably the safest way to "climb," especially because it comes with an experienced operator. While a cherry picker (which comes attached to a large truck) carries a pretty hefty hourly rate (usually at least $60–120 per hour), it does not usually take long to get a well-bonded bird if the bird's favorite person is allowed to actually go up in the bucket to the bird.

Avoid the use of water hoses in bird recapture as they are not effective either at grounding the bird (a wet bird can fly) or at "herding" the bird to lower branches (because most hoses have such a short, limited range). Those enormous "Super-soaker" water guns that can shoot up to 50 feet (14.5 m) are much more effective at coaxing a bird from one branch to another. While it may not be possible to coax a bird all the way to the ground in this way, a bird can sometimes be moved from tree to tree until it is in a tree that can be climbed or accessed with a cherry picker.

Capturing Established Feral Parrots

Wild-caught, poorly socialized, or established feral parrots might have to be trapped. This is also typical of small, good flying birds. Especially during late summer or early fall, there may be sufficient ripe fruits to sustain the bird in the wild for quite some time. If there is food readily available in the area, a parrot will probably be more difficult to recover.

The dish is moved progressively lower until the bird must enter the cage to get it, and a human waiting out of sight pulls the door closed with a wire. (Quaker parrot)

Begin the process of trapping a bird by establishing a food dependency. If the bird is spending the same block of time every day in the same place, such as in a fruit tree in your yard, take the time to construct a feeding station. Do this when the bird is away from the area so that it will not become overly wary of humans and things touched by humans. Put food on a white surface, maybe a sheet, towel, or board painted white. This helps the bird to see the food.

If the bird is spending time in a fruit tree, it will be looking for additional "fruits" as the tree's fruit ripens and then disappears. Save some of the good fruit in the refrigerator so that as the tree's fruit wanes, the same fruit can appear on the feeding station with the "new" foods we are using to entice the bird. You may put fruits from the tree on the feeding station, but more appealing foods might be necessary. Try corn, pomegranates, grapes, and nuts (both in and out of the shell). Some birds will come to seed, as many feral exotics survive through the winter from bird feeders intended for native species.

Once you have observed that the bird comes readily to the feeding station, you may set up a trap there, either a manufactured one (sometimes available from local human societies or animal control) or a homemade one (made from a bird cage). A cage trap (see illustration) involves providing a moveable shelf for the food, then gradually moving the shelf down so that the bird has to enter the cage to get to the food. Then a person waiting just out of sight can pull the door closed with a long thin wire (a curious parrot-type bird being trapped will probably chew through a string before it goes into the trap). While it may take weeks to establish a food dependency, it might take only minutes to trap a bird that is already food dependent.

Ethics of Recapture

Whether it is your bird or somebody else's bird in your backyard, there are several ethical reasons to persist in recapturing the bird. First, most parrots will probably be sorely pressed to survive cold winters. While it is certainly possible and has been done many times before, it is difficult and represents discomfort and possible death for the bird. Additionally, while an escaped exotic bird represents a threat to native species, consuming food meant for them and taking their space, the native raptors, coyotes, and all manner of humans represent an ever present threat to the bird. In most cases, it is probably best to recapture any solitary feral exotic bird. Just keep trying. It is easier than fishing; it is only a matter of time until you figure out how to be smarter than the bird.

In some cases, it might be considered more "humane" to allow older established ferals that have found flocks to live wild. This seems reasonable in the case of Quaker parrots, nanday and cherry headed conures, Senegals, and other small escaped exotics that have formed a few small flocks around the country. While the small numbers of these birds mean that they, themselves, do not represent a threat to the habitat, their ability to reproduce forms a potential threat. In these cases there might be some justification to trapping and spaying and neutering before rerelease. While this is not humanely feasible at this time, I envision a possible future in which the birds could be rendered chemically sterile, allowing the ones now established to live their lives wild without causing irreversible damage to native ecosystems.

Chapter Six
Stories

Portia Got the Part

The Denver Chamber Orchestra and Opera Colorado were to perform *Amahl and the Night Visitors*, a story set in the Holy Land and relating to the birth of Jesus. The script called for a parrot in a cage. Could I supply one?

The answer was a qualified "Yes." My favorite, Portia, was available, but being a New World bird, his species could not have attended the birth of Jesus in the Middle East. Muffin, my cockatiel, was also an impossible candidate for similar historical and geographical reasons. My only Old World parrot, Tom Foolery, a lovebird, was too small to be seen on stage.

It was time to acquire that African ringneck I had wanted for so long. A local pet store had ringnecks in stock; armed with my checkbook I was there within the hour. The remaining bird was rather disappointing—in poor feather, with no trace of a ring around its neck. I decided to look further and called a friendly wholesaler who, I hoped, could refer me to a retail store with ringnecks.

"I don't know anyone," he said, "but I have a pair, and the one I thought was a female just developed color. I'm looking for someone with a female to trade for a male."

It was time to talk turkey. I bought the colorless specimen and traded her to the wholesaler for his lovely rose-ringed male in perfect feather.

An old British parrot book confirmed that ringnecks were highly prized during the time of the Roman Empire and that they were kept in "ornate cages." I was convinced that I had found the perfect bird for the opera *and* the perfect cage. The evening of dress rehearsal I delivered the African ringneck in a tall, square wrought iron cage with a domed top. It was lovely, but it weighed about 25 pounds.

I didn't know that the page who was to carry the bird also had to carry a lantern, a staff, a sack, and a carpet. I also didn't know that he had to carry them through the audience from the back of a large two-story hall. The ringneck wound up in a small budgie cage.

Adding insult to injury, the director complained that the bird was too

Portia, always a singer with an eye for the ladies, was in poor feather in his twenties. **(Amazon)**

small and was not really what they had in mind. The bird the producer described—the bird the producer wanted—was an Amazon.

Authenticity was the loser; I was asked to provide a parrot from a part of the world unknown until about 1500 years after the time of the event!

I explained that Portia loved singing, and that he might break into any one of several "rolls" during the performance. He has a large vocabulary, including such favorites as "Oh, what a pretty bird!" (running 5 to 15 minutes); the "Clean up your cage/Shut-up!" interchange (audible for several floors of my apartment building); and "Somewhere Over the Rainbow" in off-key falsetto.

The risk of being upstaged by a parrot was a small price to pay for such a fine bird. Portia was the bird the producer wanted; Portia was the one he got.

The parrot in *Amahl* and its slightly hard-of-hearing owner provided comic relief in the inspirational story. Portia had only two responsibilities—to take food (a role my slightly obese parrot was born for) and to be quiet. I wasn't so sure about the quiet part.

The opulent production took place on two cold December nights in the beautiful Trinity Church, a national historic landmark. The sanctuary is a masterpiece of turn-of-the-century woodwork and stained glass. Enormous brass organ pipes formed a gleaming backdrop for the stage, the esteemed maestra JoAnn Falleta, and her orchestra.

Waiting in darkness backstage, Portia was nearly perfect. A few times he inquired quietly, "What?" but he spoke so softly that only I could hear him.

On stage, too, Portia was perfect the first night, accepting food and eating it quietly. But that was just the first night.

The second performance was not sold out, and I managed a seat in the audience with a friend. As the royal procession entered, I knew to expect trouble. As the page wobbled his way to the stage, we could see that the cage was not completely covered! I braced myself for the worst.

My friend kept saying "What did Portia say?" and "I'm sure he said something." But alas, I did not hear him. My untrained ear had missed Portia's faux pas.

No, Portia didn't break into "Somewhere Over the Rainbow"; he didn't scream "Shut up!" at the tenor. But members of the orchestra reported that when each of the kings knocked on Amahl's door that cold Christmas night, a sweet, clear parrot's voice called out—on all three occasions—"Come in."

Redheads, Blondes, and "The Thunderbolt"

Parrots have some striking idiosyncrasies that seem more human than traits documented in other companion animals. For one thing, parrots put a lot of stock in hair color. It is not uncommon to encounter a parrot who will either attack people with red hair or court them. The same is true to a lesser extent of blondes; I have found that Amazons in particular seem inordinately attracted to blondes.

The attraction to hair color, however, is not nearly so curious as the parrot's predisposition to fall immediately, completely, head-over-heels in love at first sight. This phenomenon is called "The Thunderbolt." I have seen it in intelligent, well-socialized, bonded parrots such as my own yellow nape. It has also been documented in African greys, macaws, most common companion Amazons, cockatoos, and even lovebirds, cockatiels, and budgies.

This is the way it happened with Portia.

Once, during a move to a new home that was not yet ready, Portia (my life companion yellow nape), Moan Eek (my hand-fed Dutch blue lovebird), and I stayed briefly with our friend June in her downtown duplex. It was summer, and I was sunbathing on the front lawn with a book, a cool drink, and my cordless phone. Portia, not comprehending that there was no shade outside, was letting me know in no uncertain terms that he was not pleased to be left inside. The front door was open, and Portia was screaming at top volume including few words except an occasional "Shut up"—which sometimes sounded a little like "Help."

Suddenly, inexplicably, Portia was quiet. I heard the front door bang hard against the wall. Rushing into the living room I found a striking, athletic blonde woman with dark-rimmed glasses standing beside Portia's cage holding a baseball bat in a very threatening posture.

"I thought someone was being attacked," she said with an expression somehow combining relief and disbelief; "I thought June needed help!"

I explained that the birds and I were staying with June for a few days and apologized for disturbing her day.

Portia was immediately smitten—begging, twirling, pinpointing, fanning his tail, spreading his wings in full display.

June's neighbor was an accountant who worked at home. She introduced herself and went back to work. Portia and I went on about our business and forgot the incident—or so I thought.

A few weeks later, on the Fourth of July, June decided to give a party, and the neighbor was invited. Portia and I arrived early to help with food. Portia took his position on a very high curtain rod in the nonsmoking room. By the time the blonde neighbor arrived, the room was crowded, but Portia instantly acknowledged her entry with a loud scream. Of course, the neighbor had to tell the story of the beautiful parrot who was nearly attacked—or maybe rescued from boredom—with a baseball bat.

I took the opportunity to encourage Portia to entertain the crowd with his rendition of "Somewhere Over the Rainbow." As he pinpointed, displayed, and postured in the direction of the beautiful woman with whom he was smitten, I said, "Portia, sing for us."

Instead of launching directly into his usual off-key falsetto, Portia, eyes flashing like a Las Vegas casino sign said, "Portia, sing for us!" Then he sang "Somewhere Over the Rainbow."

Portia and I had a marvelous relationship, and he was devoted to me; but I know if he had had a choice at that party, he would have gone home with June's blonde neighbor.

From that moment on, those words became a permanent part of Portia's riff. He is mated now, but if the moment is right and the mood strikes him, he still says, "Portia, sing for us" before he sings "Somewhere Over the Rainbow."

I sometimes fancy that Portia thinks of his "lady love lost" when he repeats those words today. More likely, he is merely singing a "song" he learned when he was trying to impress June's beautiful blonde neighbor by repeating those words he had learned to say *the first time he ever heard them.*

Into the Aftermath

Nightmares didn't wake me last night as they did so often the year of the hurricane. To say I was affected by walking through Katrina's rubble is an understatement. Who wouldn't be? We found some birds in time and moved them to safety; we also found tragedy. I'm comforted by the memory of a rooftop on Treasure Street—a vision of empty cages, doors open wide, and evidence of birds returning to eat and drink in the massive muddy wasteland that once had been Louisiana's eastern coast.

The Gathering Storm

As the historic weather event crossed Florida and approached through the northern Gulf of Mexico, one nearby family agreed to keep a friend's birds as he evacuated. Donna Powell's Baton Rouge suburb proved far enough from Katrina's eye—80 miles northwest of New Orleans—to ride out the storm, yet close enough to serve as convenient, temporary shelter for just a few feathered friends of friends. Besides, Donna Powell loves parrots and had recently founded a service, *911ParrotAlert.com*, to help reunite lost pet birds with their people under "normal" circumstances. Soon things would be well past normal in Baton Rouge.

That first appeal for help was followed by many more. As the most destructive natural disaster in United States history stalked the Gulf Coast, Donna's telephone and doorbell just kept ringing. The city of New Orleans, 80 percent below sea level, was forced to evacuate. Friendly requests became desperate pleas for pets needing shelter

Many parrots, just like this red-headed Amazon, were saved in the wake of Hurricane Katrina by dedicated volunteers.

as their owners evacuated. Donna's sprawling ranch-style home was about to become the busiest emergency parrot rescue operation in history.

Internet Clarion Call

On September 9, 2005, I received an e-mail reporting that the Humane Society of the United States was requesting volunteers with vans and up-to-date hepatitis and tetanus vaccinations to retrieve animals from the abandoned city. A special call went out for volunteers experienced with "spiders and birds." We were instructed to bring boats (if possible), waders or high rubber boots, insect repellent, sunscreen, batteries, flashlights, and gasoline. We would need lots and lots of dog food. Among the many facilities needing assistance was Donna Powell's 911ParrotAlert.

I seemed a pretty fair candidate to serve: vaccinated, no time clock to punch, and a new white Grand Cara-

911ParrotAlert volunteers and a New Orleans police officer laugh with relief at the sounds of live birds.

van. Baton Rouge was a "mere" 13-hour-drive from my home. How could I *not* go? In two days my van was packed inside and out with a portable aviary, hundreds of pounds of dog food, cat food, bird food, gasoline, sanitary supplies, and my 22-foot fiberglass ladder. I left home to work for Donna Powell's 911ParrotAlert on 9/11/2005.

Baton Rouge Bulges

I arrived nearly two weeks after the last levee failed. The Louisiana capital, Baton Rouge, usually an easy commute from the Big Easy, was flooded with cars and people. Refugees from the storm had been followed by military, FEMA, medical and towing teams, utility workers, and volunteers. Limited space, supplies, and services igniting high voltage tempers complicated all aspects of life. Everything took time,

lots and lots of time. Simply buying gas could take hours—if you could find gas.

I reached the Powell residence around 3 A.M. on September 12, had a brief tour, and was introduced to anyone still awake at that hour. Gail Hale of Aussie Bird Toys, Bellevue, Washington, was there with her friend, Janelle Zurko. Nell and Larry Knapp of KnappTime Adoption, Rescue and Education, Warren, Michigan, were there, too. Dr. Julie Burge returned to Kansas City that Monday. We would be joined by Texas volunteers, John of Beaks and Wings and Veterinarian Dr. Lori Trajan with two technicians (one her husband). Later Dr. Fern Van Sant of San Jose, California, and Dr. Greg Rich of Metairie, Louisiana, would prove invaluable at the shelter. I remember the faces and hard work of many other brave, significant volunteers whose names I can't access at this moment.

That first night I napped on a den sofa until 6 A.M., when the phone started ringing. Donna's home came alive in every nook and cranny. The dining room housed small birds, the patio large hookbills; the breezeway, bedrooms, bathrooms, and halls were lined with bird cages, supplies, and human volunteers. Neil's bedroom was home to the occasional hamster or mouse. I don't know where they kept the snakes. One back hallway became an avian veterinary care unit, complete with refrigerated medications. Some birds were quarantined, and the portable outdoor aviary housed finches and other softbills.

Conditions were less than ideal, but volunteers at the Powell home probably had it easier than most. Hundreds of huge, state-of-the-art motor homes, minivans, Airstream trailers, SUV's, and pickup trucks with plywood campers appeared at Lamar-Dixon/Gonzalez shelter almost hourly from all over North America. The concrete and sheet metal facility had many stalls designed for livestock exhibition. Although Lamar-Dixon was reasonably spacious and reasonably well equipped, it was quickly overwhelmed by sheer numbers of lost pets and the people caring for them.

Although they were probably given at least one meal daily, sometimes from a table by the side of the road, many chubby volunteers would go home slimmer after the "Katrina diet." In areas where utility service could not be provided, free bottled water stations were much in evidence. Our group usually had a big pot of something bubbling on the stove so that we could grab a bowl whenever possible. We were introduced to all manner of strange and wonderful Cajun fare; chicken, sausage, shrimp, crab, even crawfish gumbos. Sometimes the food nearly made up for the extraordinary expenses—the love bug guts stuck all over our vehicles, the redundant flat tires—for the stench, humidity, and iffy sleeping accommodations. IF you had time to sleep, you might or might not find a place to lie down. IF space on a bed or sofa or mattress or the floor was available when you happened to finish work (or collapsed from exhaustion), that is where you slept. Those who retired earlier had a better chance to claim something truly horizontal. As a night owl, I usually ate between 9 and 11 P.M. and then slept on the floor or, if I got lucky, a sofa. After the Knapps left September 18, I joined Janell and Gail in staking out sleeping places in a real bedroom.

Many of Donna Powell's neighborhood trees had lost limbs; homes only yards away from hers were damaged. But Donna's house stood sound and functional with water and sewer service even during power interruptions. A mountain of donated cages and toys arrived from generous individual and corporate supporters. Flood waters had

One of many beloved compaion parrots we could never find was a baby black-headed caique.

come quickly. Transportation had been dear. With so many having to leave so much behind, it was comforting to know the birds would be reunited with their owners in new cages, with new perches, toys, supplies and accessories. No birds were removed from Louisiana, as our primary focus was helping those who had to leave birds behind find their pets easily in one central location—911ParrotAlert's Baton Rouge facility.

On the Job

My first task that Monday morning was tending the entire shelter, including answering a non-stop telephone while all other volunteers transferred birds from LSU. I was frankly terrified, having to find and administer medications after so little sleep. Fortunately, the 911ParrotAlert staff returned midday with many helping hands and 40 or so small birds from Parker Coliseum, the triage location for

Louisiana State University School of Veterinary Medicine.

I alternated days on and off-site, working one day at the overcrowded avian refugee camp that was Donna's house, the next day with crews retrieving animals from the silent toxic wasteland that New Orleans and its suburbs had become. Signs on our vehicles read "911ParrotAlert," "KARE Emergency Rescue," and "Positively Parrots," among many represented organizations. Because of restrictions on access to the city, we were careful to have everything in order as we approached any checkpoint. FEMA blocked all major thoroughfares into the city. On September 13 and every day thereafter, we drove off the freeway and right back on if we explained our mission to local authorities. Louisiana Highway Patrol and military checkpoints always allowed us to pass, sometimes with directions to bring out a particular animal, sometimes with an escort.

Anyone could see we were there for the birds, but we worked with almost any animal in trouble. As we often told the omnipresent young soldiers standing guard over miles of abandoned properties still inhabited with pets, "Sure, we'll help with that dog," or, "Of course, we're equal opportunity rescuers." My van transported three blue-and-gold macaws, one umbrella cockatoo, and several cockatiels, budgies, and finches; but also many dogs and cats, one large African cichlid, several gorgeous constrictors, a

couple of tortoises, and half a dozen show or gamecocks.

Mobile phone service in New Orleans was even more undependable than our sleeping arrangements in Baton Rouge. Simply getting from one address to another remained problematic because so many streets were flooded or otherwise impassable, and most service stations had long since sold out of New Orleans street maps. We noticed that utility and military personnel had a ready supply of maps, so Dahlijah Rahm, a volunteer from Canada, offered to give one soldier a foot massage in exchange for his extra map. We didn't have to go without maps after that. On Saturday, September 17, we began working closely with Pasado's Safe Haven animal rescue from Seattle. After we agreed to take a fish they found, Posado's volunteers marveled at our skill in moving an umbrella cockatoo stresslessly into a transportation cage, and we began meeting with them at the end of every day to exchange our dogs and cats for any birds, snakes, and turtles they might have found. This saved us the hours-long drive and line into Lamar-

Dixon—where we might wind up being turned away—and saved them a trip to Baton Rouge.

On days at the shelter I transported volunteers to and from the airport, ran errands, made constant repairs, and hosed down carriers, cages, and other equipment for retrieval teams. We all changed flats and helped start cars, as simply keeping our vehicles running proved an expensive challenge. Ubiquitous broken glass and metal debris flattened tires daily and humidity sapped the strength from even new batteries.

Rick Jordan stopped by with the American Federation of Aviculture truck. After coordinating our inventories, 911ParrotAlert volunteers quickly loaded more onto the truck than they removed. The truck immediately headed east toward Mississippi to deliver necessary supplies directly to affected aviculturists.

Just as animals constantly arrived, they were also constantly leaving. One day a charming nurse came for her cockatiel, Quaker parrot, and mouse (which entered our shelter in a paper bag.) As we loaded the birds' new cages, food, and toys, I watched Neil send the rodent home in a beautiful purple Habitrail donated by Petco. The owner had been working, on duty as a nurse, when everything went to dirty-water-no-plumbing-no-electricity-no-phones heck. Unable to leave her post even though her own home was flooding, she was ecstatic to find her pets safe.

Unexpected Lesson

This trip to Louisiana turned out to be much, much more than an exercise in volunteerism. Those open cages on Treasure Street forced me to reconsider trimming wing feathers.

For many years I had advocated wing trims for companion parrots for safety reasons, but I increasingly counseled careful clients to improve their birds' quality of life by allowing flight. Now it was time to reexamine my assumptions about safety. Although in-home confrontations with sinks and toilets, ceiling fans and swinging doors kill and maim many pet birds, these accidents might be equally preventable in birds with flight ability. Now it was time to counsel better indoor flight safety, flight training, harness training, and retrieval techniques, rather than reach for the scissors. Yes, in some circumstances trimming wings might be good, but I now see that flight may be the better option.

Rising waters in Katrina's wake left many people running for their lives with little or no time or resources for others, even for their own pets. Many locals lost their lives trying to stay with and defend in-home businesses. Kudos to those on Treasure Street and others who had the faith and optimism to release their birds. Some of those pet birds will be recaptured. Others will naturalize, becoming a wild, living part of Louisiana's lush environmental melting pot.

Glossary

Please note that the following definitions set forth the meanings of these words as they are used specifically in this text. They are not intended to be full and complete definitions.

abandonment: the feeling of being left behind and out of the flock. To a parrot this can mean death.

adaptive behaviors: learned behaviors that increase the bird's chances of surviving (producing more offspring).

aggression: hostile nipping, biting, or chasing.

allofeeding: mutual feeding or simulated mutual feeding. One of several behaviors related to breeding.

allopreening: mutual preening or simulated mutual preening, as in a human scratching a parrot's neck.

anthropomorphic: ascribing human attributes to a nonhuman creature.

aviculture: the practice of keeping and breeding birds and the culture that forms around it.

baby days: a young parrot's first, impressionable weeks in the new home, an idyllic period before the baby bird's instincts for independence, dominance, and exploration develop.

band: coded metal device placed around a bird's leg for identification purposes.

beaking: testing the feel of the beak on various substances, including skin, by a baby parrot.

behavioral environment: behavioral conditions, especially redundant behaviors including habits, present in the bird and in individuals around the bird.

bite: use of the parrot's beak in a manner intended to cause damage or injury.

bite zone: area in front of the bird's beak in which the hand can easily be bitten but not easily stepped on.

blood feather: unopened feather that is completely or partially covered by a bluish/white membrane indicating that the feather is currently supplied with blood.

bonding: the connection with another bird, a human, an object, or a location that a bird exhibits and defends.

breeding-related behaviors: behaviors with a source related to breeding habits in the wild, such as chewing, emptying cavities, hiding in dark places, allopreening, allofeeding, masturbating, copulating, and aggression at the nest site (cage).

cage bound: so fixated on an unchanging environment that any change stimulates either aggression or fearfulness in a captive bird.

cavity-breeding behaviors: describes breeding-related behaviors of parrots, including chewing, emptying cavities, fondness for small spaces, peeking out, and aggression at the nest site.

chasing: to drive away by pursuing.

cloaca: also called the vent. Part of birds' anatomy where waste materials are collected for excretion. Also, opening where sperm or eggs are transmitted.

command: an order or instruction given by a dominant individual.

companion bird: a bird that lives compatibly with humans.

contact call: the word or sounds the bird greets all "flock members" with, such as, in a companion parrot, "hello."

contours: the layer of feathers on the breast and body that cover the down.

coverts: the layer of feathers protecting the base of the primary feathers of the wings.

counterintuitive: going against intuition.

crest: a set of feathers on the head used for expression of emotions in the cockatoo.

defensiveness: occasional, mild, or infrequent territorial aggression.

developmental period: a period of rapid behavioral development wherein a parrot might demonstrate tendencies for dominance, independence, aggression, and panic. (See also: "terrible two's.")

dominance: control, enforcing individual will over others.

down: the small fuzzy feathers next to the body that are normally covered by contours.

drama: any activity that brings an exciting response, either positive or negative.

"evil eye": A behavioral technique in which the bird is stopped from unwanted behavior by a stern, predator-like two-eyed gaze.

eye contact: the act of maintaining eye-to-eye gaze.

family: The Order of parrots, Psittaciformes.

feather tracts: symmetrical lines of circulation along which feathers grow, molt out, and regrow. This incremental replacement of feathers gives balance to the bird in order to maintain flight ability during molting.

feral: previously captive animals living wild in habitats where they are non-native.

fight-or-flight response: instinctual, automatic reaction to real or perceived threats.

fledging: the process a young parrot goes through as it learns to fly for the first time.

flock/flock members: as it applies to a companion bird, human companions sharing a home with a captive parrot.

forage: the search for and consumption of food.

good hand/bad hand: a behavioral technique designed to distract a bird from biting (see page 48).

grooming: the process of having the companion parrot's wing feathers trimmed, nails cut or filed, and beak shaped, if necessary.

habit: redundant behavior that has become a fixed part of the bird's behavior.

hand-fed: a parrot that as a neonate was fed by humans rather than birds.

handling techniques: methods used by humans to stimulate and maintain successful tactile interactions with companion parrots.

hookbill: a parrot.

human/mate: the human companion chosen by the bird to fill the role of mate. The bird will perform courtship displays for this person and protect this person as it would a mate of the same species.

imperfect: a bird with an obvious physical defect resulting from congenital anomaly or injury.

independence: improvising and enjoying self-rewarding behaviors.

juvenile: immature behaviors unrelated to nesting or breeding.

language: a method of verbal communication wherein multiple individuals use the same sounds or groups of sounds to convey the same meaning.

mandible: the lower beak, horny protuberance with which the bird bites against the inside of the maxilla.

mate: the individual to whom the parrot is primarily bonded. (See also:human/mate.)

maxilla: the upper beak; the notched protuberance that gives the hookbill its name.

mimicking: to copy modeled behavior, especially vocalizations.

model: A learning process by which one individual copies behavior from another individual.

molt: The cyclical shedding and replacing of feathers.

nest/nesting: the act of constructing a structure for the purpose of reproduction.

nest box: a human constructed box for bird nesting.

nipping: an accidental, unintentional, or nonaggressive pinch not intended to cause damage.

night frights: unexplained thrashing in the night that is sometimes seen in cockatiels and some other companion parrots.

parrot: a hookbill; a bird with a notched maxilla, a mallet shaped tongue, and four toes (two facing front and two facing back).

patterning: a learned habit. Establishing cooperative behavioral patterns with the use of interactive drills performed by birds and humans together.

pecking order: the hierarchy of dominance within a group of birds or their companions.

pinch: a behavior designed to get a human's attention where the bird takes that person's skin in its beak and squeezes hard enough to cause pain but not hard enough to break the skin.

preen: to groom the feathers, as with "combing" and "zipping" them with the beak.

prompt: a cue, the physical cue to used to stimulate a behavior.

Psittaciformes: the parrots.

quarantine: enforced isolation for the prevention of disease transmission.

recapture: to apprehend or recover possession of a parrot that has flown away.

regurgitate: voluntary or involuntary production of partially digested food from the crop. (See also: allofeeding.)

reinforce: process of rewarding a behavior that we wish to become habitual.

reprimand: punishment; action intended to discourage a behavior.

rescue: fortuitous removal from frightening circumstances.

rival: a competitor, one who competes for reinforcement or reward.

roaming: unsupervised explorations away from approved cage or play areas.

roost: the place where a bird usually sleeps.

self-rewarding behavior: an activity that is enacted solely for the pleasure of doing it.

sexual behavior: self-rewarding breeding-related behavior.

sexual maturity: the period during which breeding-related behaviors become prominent in the bird's overall behavior.

species: subgenus; related groups of individuals that share common biological characteristics.

status: positioning related to dominance within the pecking order.

step-up: practice of giving the step-up command with the expectation that the bird will perform the behavior.

stress: any stimulus, especially fear or pain, that inhibits normal psychological, physical, or behavioral balance.

subspecies: a subdivision of species, especially by color or geographical characteristics.

substratum: material placed in the bottom of the bird's cage or play area to contain mess and droppings. (pl. substrata)

"terrible two's": a behavioral period wherein the bird's instincts for dominance, independence, and aggression are first manifest. (See also: developmental period.)

tool: an implement that is manipulated to accomplish a particular function.

toxin: any substance that causes illness or death through exposure to it.

toy: any tool for producing self-rewarding behavior.

treading: the style of mounted copulation used by most parrots.

vent: cloaca.

vocabulary: words or elements comprising a language.

weaned: when a baby parrot has learned to eat independently.

window of opportunity: a finite period during which something can be accomplished, a period of time during which behavior can be changed.

wobble distraction: a behavioral correction performed during step-up practice (see pages 47–48).

wound up: when a bird is obviously excited and could bite unpredictably.

Information

Organizations
American Cockatiel Society, Inc.

American Federation of Aviculture

Association of Avian Veterinarians
P.O. Box 811720
Boca Raton, FL 33481

National Cockatiel Society

International Parrotlet Society
P.O. Box 2547
Santa Cruz, CA 90063

Magazines
The AFA Watchbird

Bird Talk
P.O. Box 6050
Mission Viejo, CA 92690

Positively Parrots.com

BJWHF.com

Parrot

Books

Athan, Mattie Sue: *Guide to the Quaker Parrot,* Hauppauge, NY: Barron's Educational Series, Inc., 1997.

Athan, Mattie Sue and Deter, Dianalee: *Guide to the Senegal Parrot and Its Family,* Hauppauge, NY: Barron's Educational Series, Inc., 1998.

Low, Rosemary: *The Complete Book of Parrots*, Hauppauge, NY: Barron's Educational Series, Inc., 1989.

Vriends, Matthew M., Ph.D.: *The New Cockatiel Handbook*, Hauppauge, NY: Barron's Educational Series, Inc., 1989.

Wolter, Annette: *Parrots*, Hauppauge, NY: Barron's Educational Series, Inc., 1992.

Index